Clear Thinking about Sexual Deviations

James L. Mathis

**Chairman
Department of Psychiatry
Medical College of Virginia
Virginia Commonwealth University**

**Nelson-Hall Company
Chicago**

Clear Thinking about Sexual Deviations

ISBN: 0-911012-40-0

Library of Congress Catalog Card Number: 72-80165

Copyright © 1972 by James L. Mathis

All rights reserved. No part of this book may be reproduced in any form without permission in writing from the publisher, except by a reviewer who wishes to quote brief passages in connection with a review written for broadcast or for inclusion in a magazine or newspaper.

Nelson-Hall Company, Publishers
325 W. Jackson Blvd., Chicago, Ill. 60606

Manufactured in the United States of America

Although the examples in this book are based on the behavior of real people, the names have been changed, along with other significant biographical information, to protect the identity of persons living or dead.

Contents

Introduction vii

Chapter 1. The Development of Sexual Identification 1
Chapter 2. Homosexuality 13
Chapter 3. Exhibitionism 29
Chapter 4. Voyeurism 41
Chapter 5. Pedophilia 53
Chapter 6. Transvestism 67
Chapter 7. Transsexualism 79
Chapter 8. Fetishism 91
Chapter 9. Sado-Masochism 103
Chapter 10. Rape 119
Chapter 11. Incest 133
Chapter 12. Madonna-Prostitute Syndrome 145
Chapter 13. Prostitution 159
Chapter 14. Group Sex 175
Chapter 15. Miscellaneous Deviations 189

Epilogue 207

Index 215

Introduction

SEXUAL BEHAVIOR HAS fascinated man since the beginning of recorded history. It became associated with evil and sin in the Judeo-Christian culture when it allegedly led to mankind's downfall in the Garden of Eden. Centuries were to pass before this odious connection began to give way to knowledge and reason. The Dark Ages of sexuality were filled with myths, half-truths and general misinformation. Many of them remain in this otherwise enlightened twentieth century.

The present age has been referred to as a period of sexual revolution. This is not altogether true, and evolution appears to be a more accurate term than revolution. Whispers of understanding and new knowledge began in the late nineteenth century, and by the middle 1900's it was no longer possible to deny that man was a sexual animal and that the psychology of sexuality was a respectable topic for discussion.

One area of sexual behavior, that which deviated from the norm, has resisted the new attitude and approach until quite recently. The sexual deviations were so deeply associated with degradation and depravity that they became synonymous with the lowest form of vice, and seldom were they referred to without the words *fiend* or *fiendish*. It was generally assumed that they existed only among the bottom levels of the socioeconomic strata, despite massive evidence to the contrary. Long after other forms of aberrant behavior had been accepted as the product of emotional disturbance, the deviations of sexual behavior remained the acme of sin and wickedness. Only in the past few years has the subject become one of legitimate social and medical interest.

We are witnessing a worldwide attempt to substitute education and information for mythology and ignorance in the sphere of sex. Freud was defiled and ridiculed for stating that sexual interests and behavior began in childhood and persisted throughout life, but modern school systems are criticized and accused of neglect of duty if they do not have courses in sexual education in grade school. This new wave of public education is far from satisfactory, however. Many questions about sexual behavior do not have answers, and many of the answers given are controversial.

It is generally agreed that attraction between opposite sexes is normal. There are many variations of sexual activity that fall within this normal range, but there are many that are clearly pathological and are recognized as diagnostic entities by the medical profession. This book will describe and attempt to explain these diagnostic entities to the best of our present knowledge. Many of them will sound incredible to the average reader, and even psychiatrists find some difficult to understand and even more difficult to accept as human behavior.

The author's interest began as a purely clinical one. While attempting to help these emotionally disturbed people by psychiatric treatment, I became aware that the prevailing attitude toward sexual deviates was an archaic attitude of vengeance and punishment. It quickly became obvious to me that one of the major deterrants to proper treatment and to a more humane legal attitude was public ignorance. It is natural to be frightened by that which is not understood. Hopefully more understanding will remove the fear, and when the fear is gone, perhaps sexuality can find its proper context in human behavior. Then, and only then, can the pathology of human sexuality become a "legitimate" disorder entitled to treatment rather than punishment. The ultimate goal is prevention, but this cannot occur without open discussion and massive education. The problem must be viewed with logic and reason unclouded by irrational emotions if we are to continue the sexual evolution to the natural end point: a humane and just consideration of all activities that vary from the norm.

Clear Thinking about Sexual Deviations

1

The Development of Sexual Identification

SOME UNDERSTANDING OF how sexual identification is developed is essential to a knowledge of the sexual deviations. The term *deviation* implies that some aspect of an individual's sexuality deviated from the norm during the development phase. Deviations from the norm may occur for a variety of reasons, and while generalities are essential for purposes of discussion, the causative factors of individual cases can be determined only by close study of the persons involved.

It appears axiomatic that a human being is either male or female, but this is not always so. There are unfortunate individuals who are born with deformed genitalia whose sex cannot be determined by inspection. Even when we confine our discussion to individuals with normal anatomy, we find that maleness and femaleness are clearcut only in the physical sense. When we speak of the feeling or the inner sense of being male or female, we enter into a much more complex situation and one which may or may not coincide with anatomy, hormones, or chromosomes.

The core gender—the sense of maleness or femaleness—is the end result of a complicated set of attitudes, feelings, and activities of the parents and, to a lesser degree, of the total social group. These attitudes are of primary importance in deciding whether or not a given individual will sense itself as a male or as a female in adulthood. The configuration of the external genitalia (penis or vagina) is the most important and accurate somatic sign of core gender to the parents and family, and later to the developing personality. However, there are many cases in which the genitalia have been underdeveloped or malformed so that the physician has erroneously diagnosed the sex of the child at birth. These errors of nature have shown that there are several variables that may enter into the question of core gender, and they also show that somatic and psychological gender do not necessarily coincide. An infant with the chromosomes of a male (XY) and with male gonads and hormones may have external genitalia resembling those of a female. If the physician tells the parents that the child is a girl, an easy mistake to make, that infant is apt to grow to adulthood sensing itself to be a female and showing all the attributes of that sex.

Do not confuse the core gender concept, maleness or femaleness, with the concepts of masculinity and femininity. Core gender is a rather basic concept universally recognized in all cultures. Masculinity and femininity largely determine the use an individual will make of his core gender, and this is far from universal. These latter concepts vary markedly from culture to culture and from age to age and may even determine specific subcultures in a given segment of society. We are constantly redefining and modifying what we mean by masculinity and femininity.

We may simplify by saying that with few exceptions development of core gender identity appears to be derived from two major sources: (1) the anatomy and physiology of the external genitalia; and (2) the attitudes of parents, siblings, and peers towards the child's gender role. It is obvious that the second source of identity, parental attitude, usually depends upon the first, genital configurations. This may not be true, however, as the following case exemplifies.

Miss Johnson was a thirty-year-old single woman who

came to the clinic with an unusual request. She wanted to know if it were possible to have medication to coarsen her voice and to stimulate beard growth. She stated that she was a carpenter of considerable skill but that she invariably was fired from her job or was given menial tasks at lower pay when it was discovered that she was a female.

Miss Johnson was clad in a workingman's khaki shirt and pants, and with her close-cropped hair, she looked boyish. She wore a binder over relatively small breasts so that with a loose shirt or jacket her true gender was not obvious. Despite a slight body build, she could have passed easily for a twenty-year-old male. She told us the following story about why she wanted to be male.

Two sisters in a rural area had babies on the same day. One sister was married and one was single. The child of the married sister, a boy, died at birth. The unwed sister gave her married sister her child, a female, to raise as her own. The parents wanted the female infant, Miss Johnson, to replace the dead boy; so they reared her as a boy. She was given the name William, but was called Bill. There were no other children, and Bill grew up to be her father's helper on a small farm. It was a lonely life for a child, and Bill had few associates her own age. Grammar school was almost her only contact with peers, but she had little memory of these years. She vividly recalled her acute embarrassment upon being forced to wear her first dress at the age of thirteen when she entered high school.

Bill's menstrual periods began at age thirteen as a shock to her. Her mother had not warned her nor prepared her, but she quickly adjusted to the nuisance with a minimum of discomfort. Menstruation had been normal in every way after a few irregularities in the first year.

Bill finished high school as "one of the boys." She was an excellent athlete, and she bitterly resented not being allowed to compete with the boys in high school activities, especially baseball. She had no dates nor intimate girl friends, but in her senior year she became aware of her attraction to a female classmate.

It is now essential to digest a difficult concept. Bill did not become attracted to the female classmate in a homosexual sense. She was attracted to her as a boy would be attracted to a girl under normal circumstances. The fact is unquestionable that Bill had developed a core gender—a sense of maleness—that made her psychologically a male. Bill was a transsexual—an individual with a male psyche and a female body. (The reverse may be true as we shall see in a later chapter).

Bill had, by the age of thirty, established a fairly normal life as a male. She had moved to a large community where she felt that very few, if any, of her neighborhood associates knew of her true chromosomal gender. Bill was not happy, nor can she ever be, for she is literally a male trapped within a female body, and much of normal living will never be possible for her. She is socially disabled, but unlike a physical disability, her disability does not bring her sympathy or support. It brings her rejection, loneliness, embarrassment, and a sense of degradation; yet it was totally beyond her control and was irreversible before she even realized that it had happened.

This core gender—the sense of maleness and femaleness—is firmly developed by two and one-half years of age. The child who is reared unequivocally male or female for these first two and one-half years will identify permanently as such without regard for anatomy or for any subsequent events. When changes of gender assignment have been attempted in later life, and there are many such reported cases, they have resulted in confusion and emotional upset. A reassignment of basic sex after the third year should be attempted only when it can be determined definitely that the child has not accepted the role of either male or female. There are children about whom the physician has been undecided about the gender assignment, usually those with deformed genitalia, and whose parents have communicated this indecision to the children. These cases may respond to medical intervention and surgical repair after three years of age without severe emotional damage.

These observations on human beings have been corroborated by animal experiments. Dr. H. Harlow found that sexual identification in experimental monkeys depended upon two factors: mothering and association with peers. Monkeys raised without mothering, i.e., on surrogate mothers or in isolation and with no contact with monkeys of their own age group, developed no sense of sexual identity and were never able to engage in anything resembling normal sexual activtiy. They apparently could not determine whether they were male or female. Monkeys raised on the cloth surrogate mothers, but given opportunities to form normal infant-infant relationships in the early weeks of life, showed a much better ability to develop male and female sexual responses, although they still were not normal.

The studies of Konrad Lorenz indicate that many of the animals below the primates on the evolutionary scale identify immediately and indelibly with whatever impinges upon their sensory system at a certain specific time of life soon after hatching or birth. There is no evidence that imprinting, the word used to denote this phenomenon, occurs in the human being in this exact manner, but there is circumstantial evidence that certain sensory experiences may influence the development of conceptual patterns, such as core gender, in the human central nervous system. Certain of these patterns, such as the sense of maleness or femaleness, appear to remain indelible throughout life.

Now let us turn to the second aspect of sexual identity, the sense of masculinity or femininity. This is layered upon, but is not necessarily identical with, the unalterable core gender of maleness or femaleness. A female is not necessarily feminine nor is a male always masculine. The concepts of masculinity and femininity are complicated developmental processes that are culturally and socially determined and that modify and cover over the core gender but do not change it. Thus, a male transvestite may dress like a female and may have serious doubts about his masculinity, but he does not doubt his maleness at any time. He may not like being a male, but he definitely knows that he is one. His sense of maleness, core gender, conflicts with his sense of masculinity. Similarly, a homosexual female may abhor her gender to the extent of removing every outward vestige of it, but this does not alter her knowledge of her femaleness.

The development of this second major aspect of sexual identification has no clearcut beginning, ending, or guidelines applicable to all people. The most significant chronological period probably is from birth to six years of age. The core gender is already set before the age of three, but now social, cultural, and parental factors play determining roles in differentiating and establishing an individual's psychological concept of sexuality. The increased attention to the genital area noted at this age of life (the phallic period) is a mark of progressing physiological and biological maturation. The child perceives new sensations, usually pleasurable in nature, which lead to a marked increase in curiosity about its body and the body of others. Children are apt to notice that there are sexual differences and that the outline of a boy's body differs from a girl's body. This momentous discovery of the differences in the external genitalia may lead the developing child to ruminate about these differences and to concoct various explanations for them. Thus, the little girl must deal with her discovery of having no external genitalia comparable with the male. Whether or not she perceives herself as being defective or injured will depend upon, in most cases, how her mother views the role of the female and upon whether or not the mother shows a preference for that which is masculine. The attitude of her father is also significant, but it may become even more so somewhat later in her development.

The boy and girl have been equally dependent upon and attached to mother in their early years, but with the onset of these new genital sensations and curiosities, their developmental paths begin to diverge. The little boy must begin to differentiate himself from the person closest to him, his mother, and to turn toward his father. Unless he does so successfully, his future concept of masculinity may be at variance with society. There is no such necessity for the little girl to turn away from her original identification figure in order to develop an identity compatible with her somatic gender. Freud terms this developmental phase from the fourth to the sixth year of life the Oedipal period. He spoke eloquently of the unconscious rivalry that might develop between parent and child of the same sex over their love of the parent of the opposite sex. Eugene Field preceded Freud in writing about this, and in his poem "To a Usurper" he wrote with great understanding:

> To think that I who ruled alone
>   so proudly in the past
> Should be ejected from my throne
>   by my own son at last. . . .
> He trots his treason to and fro
>   as only babies can
>   and says he'll be his Mama's beau
> When he's a 'gweat big man.'

This Oedipal phase is an apprenticeship for the development of masculine or feminine identity. Core gender already has been set as male or female, but this superimposition of a sense of femininity or masculinity determines the future role as a sexual partner and parent. The most important need of this period is for the child to experience a sustained and secure relationship to mother and father figures who have maturely differentiated sexual roles in which they operate comfortably. The lack of a parent of the same sex during this phase makes it extremely difficult to establish a proper identification compatible with the core gender. The lack of a parent of the opposite sex, and this lack may be either relative or absolute, is equally discouraging to the development of adequate heterosexual relationships in the future.

Nothing in the developing child's life at this age even remotely approaches the importance of parental approval. A little girl with a harsh, demanding, and rejecting father, or from a home situation in which masculinity reigns supreme and all things feminine are deprecated, can hardly attain the desired approval by developing feminine traits. She is apt to become an adult who sees feminine characteristics not only as without positive value but also as attributes that produce discomfort and anxiety. The reverse situation for a little boy is equally harmful. The boy with a relatively masculine or overly aggressive mother and a passive father may develop a deficient sense of masculinity and become the passive-feminine type of man exemplified by Mr. Milquetoast. In extreme cases he may be so timid and impotent with women that he finds it safer to identify with them and to turn to homosexuality.

Our theoretical child enters the school years fairly assured of its maleness or femaleness and with firming ideas of masculinity or femininity developed primarily from parental sources. The next few years are used to expand and to experiment with these ideas in relationship to society, specifically the peer group. Puberty and the resultant blossoming of secondary sex characteristics offers perhaps the final chance for modification of sexual attitudes under average conditions. It is not entirely correct to do so, but puberty and the early teens might be termed the third and final step in the development of sexual identification.

We have stated that maleness or femaleness is established by the middle of the third year of life and that basic attitudes towards masculinity and femininity are firmed by the end of the seventh year. The first step appears fairly unchangeable, but the second may be modified in the early teens. Although the earlier identification as to masculinity and femininity determines largely how one views the role of the male or the female in society, the actual uses made of these identifications may depend much upon the early teen years. Just as in the years from three to six a stable relationship of a guiding and limiting nature with parents or parent figures is extremely important for both sexes, so is it in the early teens. Both sexes need to experiment with and to practice being masculine or feminine, but they need patterns to follow, and firm, flexible guidelines. The same factors that operated in the Oedipal years can now either solidify or modify the earlier concepts. There is one major exception, however; figures outside the family now assume more importance as symbols of identification than in the earlier years.

It is extremely important that parents not be threatened by the adolescent's interest outside the family. The polishing touches on the sexual identification require both boy and girl to be able to relinquish gradually and willingly the intense emotional investment in the parents. This is essential so that they may stand firmly upon their own identification with the ability to reinvest this emotional component in a mature heterosexual manner, and in a sense, someday become parents in their own right. The parents who wish to hold tenaciously to the "little boy" or the "little girl" in their children make it extremely difficult for these children to develop secure identification as masculine or feminine adults.

One of the most momentous occasions in the developing girl's life is menarche, the first menstrual period. She ordinarily will have no doubt that she is female, but if she has identified femininity as anxiety-provoking or as an undesirable way of life, the reminder of menstruation may be an undeniable one and may represent in her mind an unfortunate situation. Conversely, when the parents, particularly her mother, have seen femininity as a rather desirable situation and have communicated this to her, she may welcome menarche as a joyful sign of her coming womanhood.

It may be unfortunate that our civilization offers little support to the young people making the first faltering steps into the confusing world of adult sexuality. We glorify youth, and we overglorify sex. We have no definite puberty rite, in fact the issuance of a driver's license, and this ordinarily comes several years after the onset of puberty, is the nearest approach we make to it. Problems in the differentiation of sexual roles do not appear so frequent nor so severe in those cultures which furnish clearcut guidelines—usually ones attended with much meaningful ceremony—for full masculinity and femininity. Our society presently leaves it almost entirely to the adolescent peer group to decide upon and to establish the guidelines for that which is masculine or feminine. The advisability of this is a moot question.

Mature sexual identity requires a core gender consistent with chromosomal sex and anatomical configuration. It further requires the development of masculine or feminine characteristics compatible with the core gender and acceptable to the social milieu; and finally, the individual must make proper use of these concepts in daily living. Development may go awry at several points and in a variety of ways, but for our purposes we will consider three factors as significant in adult sexuality: the aim, the object, and the drive.

The aim of mature sexual activity is orgasm via intercourse. Disorders of this aspect may or may not be a part of sexual deviations, and certainly can occur in conditions unconnected with sexuality; e.g., severe depressions, nervous system disease, metabolic disorders, etc. The absence of an orgasmic response in the female (frigidity) may occur in an otherwise healthy individual for a variety of psychological reasons. When the aim of the adult sexual life is persistently something other than heterosexual intercourse, a deviation usually is present.

The object of adult sexual behavior is a mature individual of the opposite sex. Disorders of object include homosexuality, the choice of a same-sexed partner; pedophilia, the choice of an immature partner; fetishism, the choice of an inanimate object or a body part; and other innovations to be discussed in later chapters. Object disorders almost always represent deviations.

Drive disorders are much less definite and are more difficult to isolate. The extremes are obvious, but exact norms for sexual drive are absent. The desire or need for sexual activity is variable from person to person and in the same person from time to time. However, it is generally assumed that complete abstinence represents an abnormal situation as does insatiability as seen in satyriasis and nymphomania. Drive obviously varies with age, physical and mental condition, and circumstance, and disorders of it may or may not be associated with deviations.

The deviations to be discussed will involve one or more of the three factors listed above: the aim, the object, or the drive. Additionally, a true deviation must be patterned, repetitive, and compulsive. There is an uncontrollable urge, not responsive to reason, to seek relief from an unbearable but undefinable tension. This urge is not simply a substitute for normal sexuality, and may even coexist with a partly normal heterosexuality, although this will rarely be well adjusted. Sexual deviation is a part of, or an overt manifestation of, a basic personality immaturity.

Although some of the conditions overlap and are closely related to others, there is a distinctive pattern to the behavior in most of the deviations. This pattern of behavior tends to be repeated over and over despite dire consequences, both legal and social. It is as if the afflicted individual simply cannot learn from experience, or if he does, cannot constructively use what he has learned to change his pattern of behavior. He is compelled (compulsive) to repeat (repetitive) the same act over and over (patterned).

We will discuss sick people. Deviations are illnesses of the personality. Illnesses deserve treatment that is constructive, not punishment that is destructive.

2

Homosexuality

HOMOSEXUALITY IS EROTIC attraction to a member of the same sex. It is called lesbianism when it occurs in females, a term derived from the name of the Greek island Lesbos. Sappho, a famous poetess, is alleged to have founded the cult of female homosexual love at her home on this island. Her name has become associated traditionally with the sexual practice of cunnilingus (tongue to vagina or clitoris) which sometimes is called Sapphism. An early organization of homosexual females did honor to Sappho and her home by calling themselves the "Daughters of Lesbos," but the more modern organization is named the "Daughters of Bilitis."

Homosexuality is known to have occurred throughout recorded history in every society and culture. An ancient Egyptian hieroglyphic inscription warns the Pharaoh's soldiers not to surrender to the enemy, presumably the Hittites, for they will "be taken from the rear." The accompanying pictures leave little doubt as to what "taken from the rear" means! It is evident that homosexuality was well recognized at the dawn of written history and that homosexual rape was a fact of life not looked upon with favor by Egyptian soldiers.

The love of many of the ancient Greek men for young boys has become legendary. Plato refers derogatorily to

Socrates' relations with his young students, and eventually Socrates was condemned for "corrupting the youth of the community." (This would appear to contradict the thought that homosexuality was considered a normal, socially acceptable life style in Ancient Greece.) The homosexual component of the Greek culture was so well known that the term "Greek love" was used by the Romans to indicate the practice of anal intercourse with young boys. Many of the Caesars, namely Julius, Octavius, Caligula, and Tiberius, reputedly were active homosexuals. The tendency of subjects to mimic their rulers would lead us to believe that homosexuality was a common practice in ancient Rome. The term "Roman culture" will appear in a later chapter as synonymous with an orgy which includes all forms of sexual activity.

Many other great historical figures allegedly were homosexuals or at least had strong homosexual tendencies. Among these were Michelangelo, Shakespeare, Leonardo da Vinci, Francis Bacon, Alexander the Great, Frederick the Great, William of Orange, and many, many others. Homosexuality may be an abnormal situation and represent an emotional illness, but it in no way eliminates the possibility of productivity and fame.

Homosexuality was recognized and accepted by many of the American Indians. The homosexual male was called "Berdache" by the Cheyennes, and although he could not obtain the honors accorded to normal males, he was not ostracized from the tribe, and he was allowed to take a mate when he could find one. Most Berdache also were transvestites in that they dressed as females and functioned as such in the tribe.

Innumerable articles and books have been written about the causes of homosexuality. Many attempts have been made to show that genetic factors, hormonal imbalances, metabolic disorders, and other physical attributes lead to homosexuality, but there is insufficient evidence to support these theories.

The inheritance of a type of physique, for example, a slender, nonmuscular, "pretty" male, may make it easier to develop homosexuality, but by far the most important factor is parental attitude as was pointed out in chapter one.

Homosexual tendencies may develop when there is undue pull toward identification with the parent of the opposite sex or when there is undue pressure away from the parent of the same sex. The male who has a mother who binds him closely to her and who simultaneously derogates all that is usually considered masculine may develop homosexuality if the father figure is absent, or if he, for one of many reasons, is unable to counteract the deleterious maternal influence. The reverse situation is true for the female homosexual. Given this sort of adverse background, homosexuality may become overt when:

(a) Acting out of the homosexual impulse is encouraged by the dominant parent.
(b) Inhibitions against homosexuality are overcome by alcohol, drugs, or brain damage.
(c) Heterosexual deprivation occurs, as in prisons, nonco-ed boarding schools, and wartime conditions.
(d) The individual is placed in situations in which homosexual license and seduction are acceptable.

It must be emphasized that these factors do not cause homosexuality. They merely bring it into the open when the basic condition already is present. In most instances no such precipitating event is necessary; the condition is diagnosable in childhood.

The Mother usually receives the blame for producing homosexuals. That may be, and certainly she exerts more influence upon growing children than does the father, but a truly masculine and interested father who wanted his boy to be a man and his girl to be a woman would offset a harmful maternal influence. It is not an either-or situation, and sometimes it may be neither parent, as the following case demonstrates. Of course, even here one can say that the parents were the indirect cause because they were unavoidably absent.

Bryan was the tenth child and the only boy in a rural family. His father died before his birth, and his mother died before he was one year of age. He was raised by his nine sisters almost as if he were a living male doll. Men simply did not appear in his life until he became enamored of his basketball coach in his sophomore year of high school. This affection was returned, and a homosexual relationship which lasted for two years quickly developed. He later became a well-known college basketball player, a Korean war hero and officer, and a successful businessman, but few people knew of his dual existence. He dated women for a social front, and all was going well with him until he ran for a political office in a medium-sized city. One of his ex-lovers became angered at him over an imagined rebuff and in malignant revenge spread the word about his sexual habits. That, in a medium-sized southern town, was the end of a promising career! All of his positive attributes were forgotten quickly, and his homosexual side overshadowed all else.

Bryan's world shattered with the public revelation of his homosexuality. Future political career, job, friends, even his reserve commission in the Army, all vanished overnight. He became suicidally depressed, but fortunately he sought help and later picked up the remnants of his life in a distant city.

It is usually accepted that from 4 percent to 6 percent of males and about 3 percent of females are overtly homosexual, but the figures for females are somewhat less reliable. There is no reason to believe that there should be fewer female than male homosexuals, but Lesbianism is given far less social significance in our culture. Homosexual females may live together in fairly undisturbed harmony in most communities, but two males in a similar situation would find the social pressures greater. Male homosexuals are constant targets for the law enforcement officials in many cities, but crusades against female homosexuals are simply nonexistent.

The legal stance usually reflects the prevailing social attitude. The seduction of a boy by an older man is considered a crime against nature, and it results in heavy penalties in all states. One rarely hears a similar hue and cry raised when two females are concerned, yet there is no reasons to believe that such seductions are any less frequent. The number of homosexual seductions that occur in schools for girls is certainly equal to the number occurring in boys' schools. Occasionally one of these seductions results in the discharge of a teacher, but legal action is virtually unknown. It would seem that a sexual act lacks emotional significance unless a penis is involved!

The sexual practices of homosexuals are perhaps even more variable than are those of heterosexuals. One popular myth is that homosexual men are either male or female (active or passive) in their sexual roles. This may be true in some instances, but far more common is the practice of changing to fit the preference of a given partner at a given time. Each male homosexual may have some preferred practice, but most are quite willing and able to adapt to different roles. Anal intercourse (pederasty, sodomy) and oral genital contact (fellatio) are the two most common practices among males, but intercrural intercourse (between the closed thighs) and mutual masturbation also are practiced. Fondling and petting play perhaps even greater roles than they do among heterosexuals.

Female homosexuals (lesbians) may limit themselves to general caressing, petting, and close body contact which usually amounts to a form of mutual masturbation, but cunnilingus (oral genital) and the use of penis substitutes (dildos) also occur. The latter practice is less common than popular belief would have it, and this makes sense if the avoidance of the penis is understood to be a part of the psychological condition in female homosexuality. This myth of penis substitutes developed long before it was known that much, if not most, of the female's arousal occurs from stimulation of the external parts of the genitalia, mainly the clitoris, and not from the interior of the vagina. It is a part of the same myth that places such unreal value upon penis size. This is not to say that dildos are never used, and one vibrating penis substitute will be mentioned in a later chapter.

Another popular myth is that one can identify homosexuals by their physical appearance and mannerisms. This is true when male homosexuals attempt to dress and act as feminine as possible. Close observation shows that these people do not actually act as if they were females, but they markedly overdo it in a hysterical manner, becoming caricature of females. These men, referred to by many names such as "fairy queens" and "Mary," are the exceptions who flaunt their homosexuality as a method of attracting others. They are less mature and closely resemble in personality a severely hysterical female. At least 85 percent of homosexual males look perfectly normal and act as masculine as any other male. Some may be well-known athletes, as was a superb lineman on a professional football team a few years ago. This man never became reconciled to his homosexual condition. After having spent thousands of dollars and much of his time in unsuccessful attempts to convert to a heterosexual life, he committed suicide in his late thirties. Very few of his closest associates knew of his underlying problem.

The female homosexual who prefers the dominant, aggressive role and who acts and dresses accordingly may be called a "butch" or "bull dyke." She is the counterpart of the male fairy queen. Like him, she constitutes a small percentage of the total. The majority of homosexual females pass totally unnoticed in polite society. It is far easier for them to lead relatively normal surface lives by nature of the differences in male and female anatomy and physiology.

Whereas the male homosexual may have some difficulty in marrying and maintaining the erection necessary for heterosexual intercourse, the female has only to relax and become an apparently willing heterosexual partner. She could probably delude any male if she made a concentrated attempt to do so. She may marry and have a family, and in most instances, probably does so without arousing the suspicion of her husband even though her sexual adjustment will not be good and frigidity is apt to be her lot.

We have spoken of homosexuality as if it were a definite condition. Now we must partially refute this and further confuse the issue by saying that there is no such thing as 100 percent homosexuality or 100 percent heterosexuality. It is more accurate to think of human sexuality as on a continuum from heterosexuality to homosexuality with most people lying somewhere between these two poles. Theoretically, the individual who found himself directly in the middle would be termed bisexual. This sometimes is called "switch hitting" in the jargon of the "gay" world. While this might appear to be a rather convenient position to occupy since one could be at home in both worlds, it is not. The bisexual individual, the one who can and does function as either heterosexual or homosexual, rarely fits well in either world. This individual is not fully comfortable as a homosexual and rarely functions adequately as a heterosexual. It is probable that somewhat over 90 percent of the population is situated fairly close to the heterosexual pole, but there is sill considerable leeway for the normal individual to have certain elements of the opposite sex in his personality. Could there be such an animal as a normal male who had not internalized some of the feminine attributes of his mother?

J.H. represents a man whose position on this theoretical continuum was very close to the totally homosexual. He was born the second child of lower middle class parents in a large northwestern city. His older sister, who was mentally retarded, was almost totally rejected by their mother. During the depression years, his father worked hard and long to support the family minimally. He simply was never home except to sleep. As far as JH was concerned, his father did not exist other than as a disagreeable person who did not seem to like him. The mother lavished all her love upon her son and freely expressed her contempt for the father, whom she openly blamed for the daughter's disability. In later life JH felt that at an early age he became not only a son to his mother but also a substitute for her husband.

He recalled his mother's many seductive attitudes and habits towards him, and one particularly stuck in his mind. He remembers rubbing her back almost every night, including the upper part of her buttocks, and as he grew older, he was horrified to discover that he had an erection when he did so. He was not allowed to have his hair cut nor to wear male clothing until he entered grade school. Even then he recalls that the first haircut created a major battle between his parents and that it finally occurred simply because his father forcibly took him to a barbershop. This was one of his few concrete memories of his father and it was a very unpleasant one.

JH's father died of a heart attack when JH was approximately seven years of age. There was no other male in the family, and without exception, JH recalls no association with an adult male prior to entering high school. And yet he also recalled a very early and consistent fascination with males. When other boys his age were sneaking looks at seminude female figures in catalogs and girly magazines, he was doing the same thing with pictures of males. He liked to play with girls, and most of his high school friends were female, but his crushes were on boys, although always at a distance. He was too shy and backward to make known his affection for anyone.

JH was a very handsome, intelligent man who readily attracted both men and women. He dated girls a few times in late high school and college simply because it was the thing to do. He was comfortable with girls, but he sometimes had to work hard at avoiding physical contact that could be misconstrued as a sexual advance toward them. He vividly recalled the only time that his avoidance maneuvers failed him. He had gone to spend a weekend with a college friend at a large country place. There was a co-ed party at which the alcoholic beverages flowed freely. He had gone to bed about 3:00 A.M. pleasantly intoxicated but was not asleep when another of the house guests, a voluptuous young female, slipped into bed with him—totally nude. He became violently, physically ill and ran from the room! The very thought of sexual contact with a female was nauseating to him. At no time in his life could he recall heterosexual thoughts or even a heterosexual dream. He liked women, but only as friends and equals, not as possible lovers.

JH had masturbated almost daily since puberty and always with fantasies of men making love to him or vice versa. He fully recognized and was resigned to his homosexuality by the mid-teens, but he saw it as a degrading, abnormal thing to be viewed with shame and guilt, and he made a vow to himself that he would never yield to his impulses. His self-esteem was never high, but it sunk to a near zero when he had his first overt experience with a man when he was twenty-one. The act itself was thrilling and gratifying, but he was filled with disgust and horror the next day. He resolved never to stoop to such depths again, but this well-intended resolution lasted about one week. JH threw himself into a whirlwind of homosexual relations that obsessed him to such an extent that he soon dropped out of his senior year in college and became the kept lover of a man over twice his age.

JH's choice of partners demonstrates another factor sometimes seen in male homosexuality. He preferred his sexual partners to be older men, and he preferred to perform fellatio on them. He totally submerged his own desires under an overwhelming need to please his father-lover. During this course of his psychotherapy (he was being treated for an emotional disorder associated with, but not necessarily due to his homosexuality), it became evident that part of the meaning of his homosexual act was to ingratiate himself to the father figure in order to win his love. He came to recognize that he hated and distrusted all females because he saw them as devouring and destructive people who seduced men and made them powerless. In his unconscious he felt that his mother had destroyed his father who otherwise would have loved him. In his relationships with older men he was trying to fill the void in his life and find a substitute for a father's love and attention.

The depression for which JH eventually was treated might have happened with or without his homosexuality, but it appears to be a frequent accompaniment of the condition. JH was a brilliant man who appeared in his youth to have a great future, but periodic episodes of despondency prevented him from realizing his early promise. He drifted about the country from one menial job to another and from one aging keeper to another until his mid-thirties. He finally had a mental breakdown, received proper psychiatric care, and, at the age of forty, finished the education begun over twenty years before.

JH apparently never conceptualized himself as anything except homosexual from the day he was able to think in such terms, even though he did not accept it fully until his teens. The first dawning of awareness of homosexuality may come as a distinct shock to many others, however. Mary, for example, was a lovely young college freshman who came to a student health clinic extremely distraught. She had not been aware of any sexual attraction for males, but she had attributed this to her fundamental religious nature and to her idea that any form of sex prior to marriage was evil. This included a firm belief that sexual thoughts were just as evil as overt activity, and that they would doom one to hell. She was shocked to find herself violently in love with her college roommate and to find that her love was reciprocated. Soon they were engaging in sexual relations, a thing even more shocking to her. After the first thrill of the romance had worn off, she became overwhelmed with guilt and shame and with the knowledge that she was a "queer." She was so distraught that she literally begged for help to become a heterosexual individual. The outlook for her was good since her history revealed a stable family and a healthy childhood. Her homosexuality appeared to be like that sometimes seen in the early teens—a passing phase of an immature person.

The adage, "One robin does not make a spring," is very appropriate for teen-age homosexual acts. Kinsey felt that over 30 percent of males had at least one homosexual contact of some form during the teens. Many people think Kinsey's figure is a little high even considering the liberal definition of homosexuality he used. But we know that many people have homosexual contacts in the immediate postpubertal period which are no more than a part of the maturing process. These acts, however, can have disastrous results when discovered and mishandled by the adults. One such incident occurred in a small southwestern town when a thirteen-year-old boy and his chum were discovered by his father in a homosexual experimentation.

This young boy was rushed to the family physician who incorrectly confirmed the father's fears that his son was a "queer." The boy was treated as such by his distraught father for many months, and he gradually became deeply imbued with the idea that he was abnormal. So much did he believe this that his first heterosexual attempt ended disastrously and caused him great embarrassment, especially when the girl spread the word of his failure about the school. This disaster strongly reinforced the idea of abnormality that had already been forced upon him. He was in his early twenties and had fallen in love with a beautiful girl when he sought psychiatric help for his "sexual disorder." A few interviews discovered no personality disorder, no homosexual component to the boy, and he responded very rapidly to some relaxation treatments, which would be called behavioral therapy today. His homosexual experimentation at age thirteen was similar to that which occurs to many perfectly normal males, but its mishandling by authority figures produced great anguish and a near disaster.

This brings us to another myth about homosexuality. Many people believe that the seduction of a young teenager by an older homosexual is one of the major causes of homosexuality. Much of the social outrage directed toward the older man is based upon this erroneous assumption. That it may bring to light a highly latent homosexual tendency cannot be argued, but that it causes homosexuality simply is not true. The type of deviate sexual development necessary to produce a homosexual identification occurs at a very early age, certainly long before the teen years. Homosexual tendencies in males can be diagnosed in the late preschool years by astute observers.

The child has begun to show many tendencies of the opposite sex by this age. He is less active and less involved in peer contact than is characteristic of his social group. He tends to be a "Momma's boy" and to prefer the games of females to those of males. He likes dressing in his mother's clothes and will chose the female's role in children's games. These tendencies are variable and are not definite, but they might alert parents to review their attitudes toward the child.

Many men who are fanatically antihomosexual are unaware of the fact that they are fighting against something that attracts them at an unconscious level. They are totally unable to accept this consciously and find the very thought of homosexuality disgusting and frightening. This fanatical stance helps to keep their own potential doubts of their masculinity from surfacing. They may persecute homosexuals under the guise of righteous indignation in the firm belief that what they are doing is the right thing for society.

Latent homosexuality is a term used to designate an individual whose homosexual tendencies are not overt and who leads a superficially acceptable heterosexual life. The term indicates a certain degree of psychosexual immaturity which makes the individual vulnerable to psychic stress. He may, for example, have his defenses against the homosexual impulse weakened by close contact with males, such as may happen in an Army barracks or in a prison, and may become acutely anxious. This has been called "homosexual panic," and once it has started, even removal of the man from the noxious environment may not be enough. Psychotherapy to modify the inner fears and to prevent recurrence is indicated.

No discussion of homosexuality can ignore recent trends. A condition that could not be mentioned in polite society a few years ago now is television and newspaper material almost daily. Homosexual organizations exist openly in many cities and on many campuses. National organizations such as the Mattachine Society and One are championing the cause of the homosexual life and are trying to make it appear preferrable to the "straight" way. One article stated that homosexuality should be encouraged on a national level as the answer to population control problems! Some of their literature reports that homosexuality is a conscious choice of a way of life and that homosexuals highly resent being termed deviants or being classified as emotionally ill people. While there is much truth in what they say, and it is certainly a fact that there are many perfectly wonderful and normally functioning people in society who are homosexual, the condition is not a normal one. It would be a biological anachronism to support as normal a condition that would lead to the depletion of the species. Sexual attractiveness between members of the opposite sex is a basic need for the propagation of any animal species.

Society needs to take a commonsensical approach toward homosexuality. It is a deviation in the development of sexual identification, but it is one that is perfectly compatible with a productive life span. It is not a condition necessarily harmful to society. Although it does indicate a certain degree of psychosexual immaturity, it is not incompatible with any known occupation or position. Homosexual individuals do appear to have more neurotic disorders, especially depressions, than the average for heterosexuals, but this may be because they live in a society which subjects them to many tensions, anxieties, and frustrations that do not exist for most of their fellow men.

The homosexual, especially the male, also lives with the growing knowledge that he faces a lonely old age. Youth is valued among homosexuals more than any other attribute. The older man faces a life of "cruising" (working the streets and haunting bus stations, public bathrooms, etc.) and humiliation in order to obtain sexual partners unless he is financially able to purchase lovers. Homosexual "marriages" have an abysmal failure rate. The combination of pressure from society, guilt and shame (perhaps even unconscious), emotional immaturity, and the lack of the uniting force of children and family mitigate against lasting homosexual unions.

Homosexuality has various meanings to its practitioners. We saw that JH unconsciously sought a father figure toward whom he could ingratiate himself, and that he did this symbolically by performing fellatio on the older male. Others practice homosexuality primarily as a show of self-love. That is, they can only love something that is a mirror image of themselves—whether male or female.

To some males, homosexuality represents an intense fear of the female, who is seen as devouring and destructive if one gets too close. To another it represents a hostile gesture toward women as if to say, "I hate you, therefore I deprive you of that which I know you want." The psychiatrist knows that some elements of several of these concepts may be seen in most homosexuals at one time.

Many of these same mechanisms work in reverse for females. The penis may represent a dangerous, probably fatal, instrument to be avoided at all costs. One homosexual girl said that she saw the penis as probe that could puncture her "insides" and cause her death. Others see it as a desirable thing, but as something that they want to use themselves, not to have used on them. A true understanding of the unconscious meaning of homosexuality in any given person requires a complete knowledge of that person's life history.

Much has been written about the nontreatability of the homosexual. This depends enirely upon what one is attempting to do with them and for them. It is true that the overt and fairly fixed homosexual resists most efforts to change his sexual identification. It is not true that the homosexual individual cannot be treated just as well as the heterosexual for his anxieties, depressions, and all of the other emotional ills to which he is perhaps more prone than the average. Since most homosexuals are not overtly ambitious to be changed and since the type of psychotherapy necessary for the change is long and expensive and by no means guaranteed, conversions are uncommon. The best treatment society can offer at present is to accept the homosexual as just another person with a somewhat different style of life. Society must acknowledge that the homosexual is not so by choice. That decision is made for him before he even understands the meaning of sex, and once he does understand it, he no longer can control it. The only reasonable and humane attitude toward any form of sexual behavior is one that says that whatever two adults of consenting age and ability do in private is their own business!

3

Exhibitionism

EXHIBITIONISM (INDECENT EXPOSURE) is inappropriate exposure of the male genitalia for sexual gratification. It is implied that the exposure does not carry with it any intent of further sexual contact, but that it represents a sexual gratification in itself, or that it is a prelude to gratification obtained through fantasy and masturbation. The term *indecent exposure* is used as a synonym for exhibitionism in laws concerning this behavior. Under these laws, exhibitionism is considered indecent behavior regardless of the circumstances under which it occurs. The medical term *exhibitionism* refers to the act of showing the genitalia only when it is not a part of or a symptom of another mental or emotional condition. For example, a mentally retarded individual may expose himself simply because he does not have an awareness of social propriety and does not realize the consequences of his act. An individual who has regressed because of schizophrenia or because of a toxic brain disorder such as may occur in certain forms of alcoholism may exhibit his genitalia in a childlike fashion without any thought of sexual gratification. Neither of these examples represents true exhibitionism.

Exhibitionism has been one of the most popular of the sexual deviations from the literary viewpoint. Jean-Jacques Rousseau, a noted exhibitionist, wrote eloquently of his distressing condition. He said, "What they saw was not an obscene object, I never even thought of such a thing: it was a ridiculous object. The foolish pleasure I took in displaying it before their eyes cannot be described." The fact that Rousseau calls it "a ridiculous object" gives some insight into the exhibitionist's true attitude toward his own body.

The frequency of its occurrence is unknown, but exhibitionism is the most common cause of arrest for a sexual offense. This may be because one aspect of the exhibitionist's psychopathology appears to make him actively seek apprehension, but even when that is considered, exhibitionism is by no means a rare condition. It is seen in all socioeconomic levels of society, and although all exhibitionists have certain personality facets in common, there is no one definitive personality type.

Exhibitionism is seen at all ages, but it is predominantly a young man's difficulty. Most cases first come to medical attention in the early to mid-twenties, although a careful history will show that the condition actually began in the teens in the vast majority of the cases. Arrests for exhibitionism become quite rare after middle age, and when seen in the elderly, one should suspect that the exhibiting is a symptom of brain changes due to aging.

Many factors go into the cause of exhibitionism. The common denominator is that all the factors of parental influence and social environment have coalesced to produce a man who does not see himself able to compete equally in the male world. There is a lack of masculine aggressiveness and self-confidence and a tendency to feel markedly inferior to other men. Women are seen as more powerful and dangerous than men, and the exhibitionist is unable to handle conflicts with women in an overt "manly" manner. The exhibitionist simultaneously resents and strongly desires a female's support. He tends to be a passive and inactive man, but he may occasionally have outbursts of verbal aggressiveness toward the significant female in his life. Almost always, he is a marked underachiever in both social and occupational life. The exhibitionist is very sensitive to what he deems a personal slight or an undercutting of his self-esteem, and this is the most common provocation to an act of exhibitionism.

The importance of loss of self-esteem as the immediate cause of an act of exhibiting cannot be overstressed. For example, one thirty-two-year-old man with an important position with a major firm misinterpreted a communication from the home office to mean that they were dissatisfied with his recent performance. That afternoon he exhibited his penis to a woman in a crowded theatre parking lot. He was as shocked as the woman to whom he exhibited. He had not done this thing before. In fact, he denied that he had even heard of it by name. If his denial was sincere, it showed he had the ability to see and remember only those things comfortable for him, since it is unlikely that a sophisticated adult has never heard of indecent exposure.

The act of exhibiting has many different psychological meanings and may even mean more than one thing to the same man. It is intended to produce a show of emotion in the female, and whether this be awe, fear, disgust, or admiration, this tends to reassure the exhibitionist that he is, in fact, a man. However, it also denotes just the opposite in that it shows the woman that here is a little boy who wishes to be treated as a child and not to have mature sexual demands made upon him. It also has a self-punitive aspect to it. The act eventually leads to apprehension by the law, and the exhibitionist makes certain of this by returning habitually to the same place over and over again to exhibit. Not only does he symbolically destroy himself, but by the arrest, the publicity, and frequent legal exposure, he punishes his family. It is not unusual to lose both job and home after an arrest.

There actually is very little sexual about exhibitionism. It is more proper to term it a denial of sexuality and an attempt to escape from heterosexuality. The exhibitionist does not expose himself as a prelude to sex nor as an invitation to sexual intercourse. If the woman takes it as an invitation and shows indications of compliance, the exhibitionist will most frequently depart from the scene in great haste and embarrassment. There are no clinical reports of an exhibitionist ever pursuing the act to the point of intercourse even when his intended victim has made it very clear that she was willing. One patient went so far as to take a woman's address and phone number when she offered it, but four years later he still carried it, unused, in his billfold.

The exhibitionist rarely exposes himself to someone with whom he is acquainted or with whom he has personal contact. His choice of a stranger as an object differs markedly from the child molester who most frequently chooses someone known to him or closely associated with the family. Many exhibitionists choose the side of town farthest from their place of residence, or even go to neighboring cities when the impulse arises. One man, a school teacher, felt compelled to travel to New York City for his exhibiting, and he stoutly denied that he would ever exhibit in his own town.

The actual act of exhibiting may take many forms. There may or may not be a penile erection, but most frequently there is overt sexual excitement, at least in the younger exhibitionist. Masturbation, if it occurs at all, is most likely to be after the act itself, but may occur during it. Upon rare occasion the exhibitionist may invite the female to touch the penis, but usually no words are spoken beyond those needed to attract attention. Actual pyhsical contact with a female to whom the exposure is made is unusual, and if it does happen, it usually is in those men who prefer to exhibit to children.

The exhibitionist may "subspecialize." Some prefer to exhibit only to mature females, while others may choose adolescent-looking girls or even those who are obviously below the age of puberty. Homosexual exhibitionism is quite rare, but it does occur. (I have known only two cases.) These men, those who wish to expose themselves to other men or boys, most frequently show a much greater degree of psychosexual immaturity than do the heterosexual exhibitionists. It follows that they would be much more difficult to treat.

The childhood background of exhibitionists varies greatly, but the following generalities are most frequently seen. Mother was the true commander of the home. The father may have been absent, a drunken brute, a milquetoastlike individual, a fairly normal male—any of these, but he was perceived by the boy and his mother to be inferior to his wife. The mother may have ruled the roost by subterfuge and seduction, but by and large, she did it quite openly and simply by using her overall superiority and confidence in herself. The future exhibitionist was mother's boy. As one exhibitionist said after a long term in psychotherapy, "I learned while I was in the navy that an umbilical cord lasts for years and that it can stretch all the way around the world."

The case history of John exemplified many of these points. He was the elder of two children, and the only son. One of his earliest memories was of accompanying his mother when she met her boyfriend in a movie theatre. He recalls, as he grew older, that she cautioned him never to let his father know about these clandestine meetings, and that he was able to take fairly large bribes for his silence from her boyfriends. He later learned that his father had been aware of his wife's activities, but that he had felt powerless to do anything about them.

Thus did John get his early ideas of the relationship between men and women. He neither liked nor disliked his father; he was simply a nonentity in the child's life. John remembered an event sometime before puberty which seemed to exemplify the home life and his father's role in it. He recalled seeing his father peeping through the bathroom window at his own wife taking a shower! John felt that this was rather typical of the way his mother had treated his father, but on the other hand, he never forgave his father for tolerating this situation. It appears likely that the father had some sexual problems of his own, but he was not available for interview.

John was one of those exhibitionists who began as a voyeur (Peeping Tom). Window peeping is not uncommon in the early teens, and as a matter of fact, it is sometimes very difficult to differentiate true voyeurism from normalcy during early adolescence. However, in John's case it soon led to exhibiting behavior that continued throughout his life until he was forced into treatment by the police at the age of thirty-two.

Charlie exemplifies another interesting aspect of exhibitionism. He became a highway patrolman at the age of twenty-four after completing almost three years of college. He had been a good student, but his failure to complete school was simply a part of his life pattern of not finishing the projects he began. It appeared that he had found a home in uniform when he became a state trooper. For the first time in his remembered life he was able to go for over one year without any form of exhibitionism. Previously he did not recall having passed a single week since the age of thirteen without yielding to the impulse. He had one brief episode of exhibiting after being a policeman for one year, felt extremely guilty and remorseful about it, and then had no more difficulty for the next six months. Then an unfortunate and life-shattering thing occurred. Through an unusual circumstance Charlie's past record of exhibitionism became known to his superiors. He confessed when confronted and was promptly dishonorably discharged from the force. He rapidly reverted to his previous difficulties with exhibitionism, although now much worse, and this continued until he finally came into treatment several years later at the command of the legal authorities.

It is to be noted that Charlie either was able to control his behavior remarkedly well or that the impulses simply were not present while in uniform. This observation has been made repeatedly upon exhibitionists who have been in the armed services or on police forces. Very few exhibit at all while in a uniform, and even the worst of them is notably improved. The theory to explain this is that the uniform acts as a sublimation, that is, it openly proclaims to all that the wearer is a man, therefore he does not have to prove it by showing his penis. The ability to carry a gun, a well-known penis symbol, also is important to the man whose ego needs external supports.

Carl exemplifies another type of background that may lead to exhibitionism. His true parents were unknown and he had no identifiable living relatives, so his history prior to the age of four was confined to that which he had learned from outside agencies. It appeared that he had been abandoned at birth and that he had been bounced from one foster home to another for approximately his first three to four years. He then was remanded to a church orphanage which, according to his description, might have been directly out of a Charles Dickens novel. It was run by females who, even if one discounts much of Carl's memory, sounded like true ogres. The corporal punishment he received from these people was stern and liberally given throughout the ten years of his life with them. He recalls being severely beaten and having his hands tied to the wall in a semihanging position at about age seven or eight when he was discovered playing with his erect penis. His life was one of constant fear of the strong females who controlled him, and he had no memory of any contact with an adult male. However, he did not hate the women who cared for him, and he did not even recall ever having been angry at them! It was as if he could not possibly be angry at a power so great and so horrible—one that literally could destroy him and perhaps had done just that!

Carl ran away from the orphange when approximately sixteen, and for the next eight years until seen in treatment, he bounced from one job to another around the southwestern part of the country. He married a girl whose background was almost as pathetic as his own. He usually worked only two to three weeks at a menial job before he was forced to leave town after being caught exhibiting. And he was always caught, as are most exhibitionists. Like so many of them, he made it impossible not to be caught. Over and over again Carl kept repeating his past history and forcing some stronger power to take command of his life and to punish him. He saw himself as a complete nothing who deserved only the worst the world had to offer him, and then he appeared to go out of his way to be certain that he got just that.

This aspect, the compelling need to get caught and to be punished, is best exemplified by a twenty-four-year-old man who had been exhibiting quite openly for many months without apprehension. In what appeared to be desperation when he recounted the story in group therapy, he finally achieved his goal by exhibiting in the lobby of a large Catholic hospital during visiting hours in front of two of the nuns! It so happened that a policeman was standing only a few yards away at the entrance, and although the young man denied being consciously aware of this, it appears rather too coincidental! Other exhibitionists, not quite so blatant, merely return to the same street corner or school yard to exhibit from an automobile on which the license plate is perfectly visible. Attempts to escape almost never occur, and many hang around the scene almost as if awaiting the arrival of the police. This need to be caught and punished serves two purposes: the punishment alleviates the guilt, and it also places the man in a masculine position—a man among men. The resulting publicity, embarrassing at one level, is another way of exhibiting himself.

Exhibitionism, like all the true deviations, is a compulsive condition. The individual is compelled to exhibit in order to relieve himself of unbearable anxiety. It is not that he can pinpoint this anxiety or worry, or even that he appears to be abnormally anxious to an outside observer at the moment. It is as if he were driven by some inner force which simply is beyond his control. Once he has accomplished the act of exhibiting and has received some show of emotion from the female, there is a gratifying sense of relief and relaxation which Rosseau referred to as "foolish pleasure." This is rapidly followed by a sense of shame and guilt mingled with fear over the possibility of apprehension, publicity, job loss, etc. Even though he unconsciously, wishes to be apprehended and to receive the notoriety, he consciously wants to avoid being caught and being subjected to the embarrassment that results.

There is much about exhibitionism, and as we shall see later, many of the other sexual deviations, that reminds one of alcoholism and drug addiction. Alcoholics always sincerely believe that it will never happen again after they are apprehended and "dried out." The exhibitionist feels exactly the same way. This feeling that it "will never happen again" is so strong that it is difficult to get an exhibitionist to remain in a treatment situation for any length of time. It is frequently necessary for some relative, employer, or for the law to keep pressure upon the man at least six months in order to keep him in psychotherapy. Psychotherapy, particularly in a group, is an effective and efficient method of treating these unfortunate men. The results are good, and not only is the exhibiting aspect of their lives changed, but most frequently they make an upward movement in their socioeconomic status. They cease to be chronic underachievers, as most exhibitionists are. This upward socioeconomic movement has proven a good measure of when a man can discontinue treatment without having a relapse.

Female exhibitors, legally and clinically, do not exist. Women have no penis to show; and if they wish to exhibit their sexuality, they like to show everything except the genitalia. Even that exhibition is for the purpose of attracting the male and does not produce sexual gratification in itself. A woman who exhibits her feminine wares is not compulsive, nor is she doing so as a method of relieving unconscious anxiety. In short, the prerequisites for true exhibitionism are absent, no matter how obviously the woman appears to display herself.

Here we must include something on a form of exhibitionism familiar to many women—the obscene telephone call. This exhibiting is done by words rather than by personal exposure, but the basic personality and dynamics of the man are much the same as we have discussed.

The obscene call is made by a man who differs from the typical exhibitionist in two ways. First, he places great value on the use of words as symbols; and second, he feels even less a man than does the classic exhibitionist. He places the telephone between himself and the female, thereby making the "sexual' contact even less personal and threatening to him. His sexual "charge" comes from the response of the "victim," just as with the true exhibitionist. He desires either her wrath and disgust verbalized, or even better, for her to show interest and to return his obscene words. As will be discussed in a later chapter, he also is one of those unfortunate souls who thinks of sex and dirt, filth and obscenity at the same time.

Mike was a third-year college student who was arrested for obscene telephone calls. He was a brilliant boy with an excellent command of English. His telephone calls included every known word of sexual obscenity, plus a few of his own making. He always chose names from the telephone book at random and continued making calls until a female answered. He then would say something like, "Are you Mrs. So-and-so?" After a few second of talk designed to get her attention, he would say, "Do you know what I have in my hand?" Without awaiting her answer, he would describe his erect penis in graphic terms and enlarge upon how he would like for her to feel it. Many women would not hang up, so Mike would next ask the woman if she would place her hand on her "pussy." Most women began to berate him or hang up at this point, but some allowed him to continue on to all imaginable verbal descriptions. Mike would be masturbating during this conversation.

Mike was a quiet, handsome boy who had had almost no dates in his twenty-two years. He was the only child of an unsuccessful military father and an over-protective and demanding mother who had never let him grow up beyond infancy in his emotional dependency upon her. He both feared and hated and loved and admired women, but he could not openly express any of his feelings toward them. He had an unconscious need for a strong female to control him and to mother him, but he could not face the sexual aspect of women. To him sexual feelings toward women were dangerous and destructive, so he maintained a distance from them and substituted words for actions.

Mike showed his mixed feelings toward women by the insulting remarks he made to them. He felt that part of their power came from the sexual hold they had over men. Many men would agree with this, but most normal ones would argue that this "power" is not always bad!

Mike, like many obscene callers, also openly exhibited upon occasion. In group therapy with other exhibitionists, he used intellectual defenses and words to avoid emotions and feelings. Many months of work were spent in helping him learn that he could be a man without danger and that both men and women would accept him as such. He then began to relax his guard and to allow himself to express his true fears and desires and to learn that his hostile feelings toward a controlling mother need not be generalized to all females. He did learn this, however, and the group was pleased when Mike found a girl friend and ever more pleased when he was able to function "like a man" with her.

Exhibitionists are not harmful to others. As a general

rule, they are less prone to violence and aggression than is the average male. Exhibitionism is a harmless sexual nuisance. It should not be a crime under our criminal laws. If it is to be considered a crime, it certainly should be a misdemeanor, not a felony. Exhibitionists tend to be very good citizens. They become criminals only by process of law. Fortunately, several states have adopted this more reasonable and humane attitude. Exhibitionists are referred for treatment, not punished. (Some have facetiously said that treatment was punishment enough!)

Many authorities state that all males are latent exhibitionists; some more, some less. Fortunately for most men, there are socially acceptable ways of exhibiting, such as acting, politics, teaching, etc. We may exhibit our fancy cars, decorative and colorful ties, or other flamboyant clothing. Recent clothing styles for youth have produced tight pants which outline the male genitals. This is much less obvious than was the codpiece of Europe in the fifteenth and sixteenth centuries, however. This cotton stuffed leather or cloth ornament was worn by all stylish young swains to make it appear that the wearer possessed a penis and scrotum of monstrous size. Whether or not this sort of public display reduced the incidence of actual exhibitionism is unknown. Equally unknown is whether or not this practice attracted females!

It has been noted that the male of most animal species except homo sapiens is more colorful and attractive than the female. This serves a vital function in that it allows the male to lure predators away from the female when she is raising young, and it also attracts the female at mating time and insures the survival of the species. Could exhibitionism be a basic, biological drive in men, but one which no longer serves a function? It is something to think about!

4

Voyeurism

VOYEURISM IS A condition in which sexual gratification is obtained by surreptitiously observing a nude female or some part of the nude female body. The voyeur is commonly referred to as a "Peeping Tom," a name which is borrowed from the tailor in Coventry who peeped at Lady Godiva when she took a "bareback" (this does not refer to the absence of a saddle!) ride through the town market place. Tom was condemned for looking, but no one criticized Lady Godiva for tempting Tom beyond his limits of resistance by her exhibitionism. This type of semirational thinking is still with us and the law arrests Tom and winks at the Lady Godivas.

Voyeurism and exhibitionism may be conceptualized as the heads and tails of the same coin: looking at, or being looked at. One frequently finds that the adult exhibitionist gives a history of having practiced voyeurism at least one or two times during his early adolescent years, but it appears less common for the adult voyeur to have exhibited himself during the same age phase. Even though the two conditions are related, voyeurism appears far less frequently on clinical records and police files. This fact could be accounted for by the differences in arrest rates, since the exhibitionist must work in broad daylight and almost forces his eventual apprehension, whereas the voyeur's activity is confined predominantly to the hours of darkness, and he does not show the same pathological need to be apprehended.

One must differentiate the sexual pleasure and stimulation a normal male receives from viewing an attractive nude female body from true voyeurism. There appears to be a subtle shading from the well to the sick, but the term *voyeurism* implies that the act of looking becomes a primary method of sexual gratification and that it is not merely a pleasant experience or a prelude to sexual intercourse. The voyeur may be stimulated to orgasm simply by the process of viewing, but most frequently he masturbates simultaneously or as soon thereafter as possible. An occasional married voyeur does his "peeping" then goes home to enjoy normal intercourse with his wife. It is as if he first must assure himself of his masculinity before he can function sexually.

Most of these men require that the act be forbidden; that is, the gratification is not complete if the observation of the nude woman is perfectly legitimate, as would occur with a wife or at a striptease show. This forbidden aspect is more or less significant with individual voyeurs, but it is always present. In some it appears to be the most pertinent aspect of the condition. This is seen in men who unconsciously conceptualize the eyes as aggressive instruments so that they may symbolically assault the woman with them. There is the seed of this belief in the power of the eyes in all of us, and we betray it when we speak of the "evil eye," "putting the eye on someone," or "he looked a hole through me." A self-conscious woman may say that so and so "undressed me with his eyes."

The forbidden aspect also represents the man's basic attitude toward all sex as it relates to him. He does not allow sexual desires to come to a conscious level. He unconsciously represses sexual feelings, but the repression eventually fails, and the sexual impulses break forth in a deviated form.

A very sophisticated and intelligent man who had been afflicted with voyeurism all of his adult life told of an incident that exemplifies the importance of the forbidden aspect. While attending a convention in a distant city, he found himself with a party of men at a club at which the entertainers did a complete strip. He was neither attracted nor stimulated by the nude bodies, in fact he found them rather disgusting. In order to avoid looking at the performers on the stage, he studied a large menu. There was a longitudinal slit of about one inch in the fold of the menu, and as he held it before him, he inadventently saw the stage performers through this slit. He held it closer to his face so that it was as if he were "peeping" through a small aperture. He immediately felt sexual arousal and had an erection!

Voyeurism, like most of the aberrant sexual practices, varies considerably from one voyeur to another. Some wish to see a woman having intercourse with a man; some wish to see a completely nude female body; others desire to see a woman in the process of dressing; and there are those who wish to see only a specific part of the nude female body such as breasts, buttocks, or pubic hair. The drive also varies greatly. Some voyeurs are able to control the impulse for many months at a time, but there are others who are compelled to seek gratification several times a week. Many voyeurs are married, have children, and lead relatively normal heterosexual lives, but others are unable to relate directly to a woman at any time.

The act itself is not so variable and usually consists of looking into bedroom or bathroom windows with incompletely drawn blinds. The chosen windows usually are of strangers, perhaps even in a section of town remote from the voyeur's house, but this is not as true as was seen in exhibitionism.

On a manifest level, the voyeur is seeking sexual gratification. He may be consciously aware of the thrill he gets from sneaking through the night and of placing his welfare in jeopardy, but this is not his main motivation. The unconscious meaning of the act, while basically sexual, is far less simplistic and may not be exactly the same in all voyeurs. We have mentioned previously the possible hostile component in the aggressive use of the eyes to do that which is forbidden. As one voyeur expressed it, "It is visual rape."

Simultaneously, the voyeur is attempting to eradicate his own anxiety over whether or not he is actually a male. There are two aspects to this. One, he secretly feels that the female does have a penis, and since he identifies with the female, he hopes to see this organ and assure himself that he also has one. The other side of this coin is that he hopes to see the woman who does not have a penis and, therefore to reassure himself that he is different from her and that he does have one.

These two psychodynamic concepts would eliminate female voyeurs—and so it is. Women are not so prone as men to become erotically aroused by visual stimulation under normal conditions, and voyeurism is unknown among them. The absence of voyeurism among females may be due partly to the passive role traditionally assigned to them by society. Any form of sexual aggressiveness by females has been discouraged strongly in Judeo-Christian society for hundreds of years, and only the past generation has it become acceptable. Should the present trend toward equality of the sexes continue until no social or cultural differences exist, then we may see an equal amount of deviant sexual behavior. This is doubtful, however. It is inconceivable that the female will ever have the same basic anxieties that plague the male and make him so vulnerable to developmental deviations. Her lack of a penis may produce problems of a psychic nature, penis envy as Freud called it, but the threat of castration is an empty gesture for her. Nature already has settled that issue!

One twenty-two-year-old college student, who was such a severe case of voyeurism that he felt compelled to go window peeping at least every other night, voluntarily sought psychiatric treatment because of increasing scholastic problems. He had fallen from the honor student ranks to near failing in one year. He soon came to realize consciously that he was obsessed with the repetitive need to look for the female penis. It was almost impossible for him to concentrate in a co-ed classroom because he was constantly thinking that the girls actually did have something between their legs—it simply could not be otherwise. He was fascinated by girls who wore tight slacks. He could not by any stretch of the imagination unravel the mystery of where the genitals were hidden! He imagined that the penis existed in a retractable form and that sooner or later it would be visible. Over and over again he made trips to the library to look at the section on female anatomy in anatomical textbooks. Perhaps he had seen the same picture of the female genitalia over a hundred times, but there was the fantasized hope that the next time he would actually see the penis!

This young man began peeping in windows at about age fourteen. The impulse could be held to once every two to three months for the first year or so, but gradually it became stronger and stronger. He was apprehended several times in his teens, but no charges were filed. Since his father was in a business that necessitated frequent moves, the family rarely lived in a neighborhood for over a year at a time. About the time the neighborhood was ready to do something about his wandering about the area at night looking in windows, his family would move and he was safe.

He was engaged to a college classmate with whom he did "heavy petting." He was almost overwhelmed with a desire to put his hand between her legs, but despite her apparent willingness to allow it, he was unable to do so. "Something" prevented him from making the move his consciousness wanted so much. Was it the knowledge that he would find nothing; or was it the fear that he would find a penis there? Or both? He restrained himself from exploring his girl friend (or, more accurately, he could not force himself to do it), and confined his sexual life to daily masturbation and almost constant fantasy. Sometimes his prelude to masturbation was to stand before a mirror with his penis tucked between his thighs so that he looked somewhat like a female.

Although several factors are involved, much of the genesis of voyeurism lies in premature or excessive sexual visual stimulation in early childhood before the personality is mature enough to integrate the feelings. This can take many forms such as observing the primal scene (parental intercourse) or other exposures, as some of our cases will demonstrate. The exposure to sexual stimulation alone will not produce voyeurism unless there are other factors that produce a discomfort with sexuality and make masculine identity difficult to develop. There must be some events or situations that produce in the growing boy a fear that his penis will be amputated if he responds normally to sexual stimuli. All these factors will be illustrated in the case of Professor A.

Professor A was a thirty-five-year-old Doctor of Philosophy at a large midwestern university. He was not a campus leader, but he was one of those well-liked and dependable men who are the backbone of any institution. He had been married eight years and had two children, seven and five years of age. He somehow had heard that a psychiatrist at the student mental health clinic was interested in people with sexual problems, so he came seeking help voluntarily. It was not so much that he was unhappy with his condition or that he did not find it a gratifying way of sexual life, but he was a very intelligent person who knew that sooner or later he was going to get caught and that it would mean the end of his teaching career. He was very conscious of the fact that to continue the practice and end up in legal difficulties meant almost certain tragedy to his wife and two children to whom he was genuinely devoted.

Professor A had been practicing voyeurism since he was fourteen or fifteen; he could not remember the first time.

He had been caught twice at the very beginning, but because of his youth no charges had been made and he had no police record. He had gone window peeping an average of one time per week for at least twenty years without apprehension; a truly remarkable feat! He simply knew that his luck was running out.

Professor A was an only child. When he was five years of age, his father had dropped dead from a heart attack. His mother, a heavy social drinker prior to his father's death, rapidly degenerated into a severe alcoholic. When drunk, which was virtually every day of her life, she had a fixed habit of removing her clothing and wandering about the house totally nude. With rare exceptions, she had passed out on the divan or on the floor of the living room by the time he came home from school during the early years of his life. It became his routine to cover her and to care for her until she slept it off. He was rather large for his age and she was a small woman; so by the time he was about twelve years old, he was able to pick her up, carry her to her room, dress her in night clothes, and put her to bed as part of his afterschool chores.

The professor could not remember having had any close friends, and he had no dates until he was a senior in college. He rationalized this by saying that he could not have taken friends home because of his mother's alcoholic condition and the embarrassment to which she would have been subjected. (Note that it was *she* whom he wished to protect from embarrassment!) It did not occur to him to be resentful toward her or to blame her for his aberrant life. Further, he could not go out with girls or engage in any extracurricular activities because of his need to be home caring for the usually intoxicated mother. In any event, he became a loner whose life revolved around his mother, his fantasies, and his books, and he was devoted to all three.

The mother had long since been a chronic patient in a state mental hospital when the professor came for treatment. She was so demented that she had not recognized him in over three years, yet he never passed a week without paying her a visit. He remained deeply devoted to her and felt guilty because he could not afford to care for her in his own home or in a private institution. It had not dawned upon his consciousness that his surreptitious looking into windows for nude females was a hopeless and never ending task because he would never find what he was looking for—the nude mother of his childhood.

Professor A was rather typical of another aspect of the voyeur. He first said that his sexual adjustment with his wife was perfectly normal and satisfactory to both of them. He described an idealistic relationship between two intellectual people who were very compatible in all ways. Mrs. A verified most of this story when she was interviewed, but she was not so certain that the sexual relationship was ideal. He was perfectly satisfied with sexual intercourse once every four to six weeks, and this had been the pattern almost since the day of marriage. She preferred considerable more frequency, but she had never made an issue of it. She was aware of his problem, and she was extremely worried about what it could mean to his future and to the welfare of the family. She also felt that he could be more aggressive in both his home life and his work. He acquiesced to the wishes of others at all times, and while this gentle, passive element in his character had first attracted her to him, she later began to think that it placed an undue burden on her and the family.

Professor A left the university shortly after his psychiatric evaluation and went to a better position at an eastern college. There he entered classical psychoanalysis, and the final result is not known. It is almost certain that the analyst and Professor A found that he had been sexually stimulated by his nude mother, and that even though he had repressed this desire, he had been overwhelmed by shame and guilt. A mechanism to protect himself from that bad, lustful part of him would have been to completely deny the sexual part of him that was normal. Perhaps he felt that castration was the just dessert of one who allowed himself to have incestuous thoughts. The final and perhaps decisive factor in the tragedy of Professor A was the absence of a father figure to pattern himself after.

Professor A's personality and community image were similar to that which is seen frequently in voyeurism. He was a quiet, passive, studious man who must have appeared as an ideal husband, father, and citizen to his neighbors. There was nothing dangerous about him, and yet the Peeping Tom is considered a grave menace to the community. This misunderstanding may result in disastrous mishandling of these unfortunate individuals when they are apprehended, and most of them are caught sooner or later.

The voyeur is not looking for a way to enter a house and commit robbery or rape. He is not "casing the joint" for a future entrance. He simply is looking, and that is all he intends to do. Some may fight back if cornered and frightened, a normal reaction, but even this is the exception rather than the rule. The voyeur may be a community nuisance, and obviously no one is expected to assume that the prowler outside the window is a harmless man, but once he is apprehended and discovered to be a voyeur, punitive action is not indicated.

All voyeurs agree that their activities could be quickly and easily curtailed to a great degree if women simply closed blinds before undressing. All voyeurs also agree that an amazing number of women appear to be totally oblivious of this fact and to make the voyeur's access to his pleasure much easier for him. Unfortunately, it frequently is these same women who complain the loudest when they find that they have been observed in their dressing and other private activities. This type of woman frequently sets traps for the suspected voyeur.

One woman had reason to believe that a neighbor had

been in her yard near the bedroom window one night. She told her husband of this and they planned a trap. She leisurely dressed and undressed each night with the window shades only half-drawn while her husband lay behind a hedge with a loaded shotgun. The neighbor did not take the bait for some reason for several nights. The weather had turned cold and wet and the husband was about to give up his nightly vigil, when on the fifth night the voyeur appeared. He was held at gunpoint while the police were notified and on their way. The case became front page news in the medium-sized community, and although the court was lenient and did not punish the man, he lost his job and home and was forced, at the age of thirty-eight, to begin life anew in another area. His wife and two children, as so frequently is the case, became the innocent sufferers in this tragic drama.

Another man, somewhat younger, is an example of a different form of the premature exposure which may lead to voyeurism in adulthood. He was an unmarried postgraduate student in geology who was remanded to treatment when arrested while peeping in a neighborhood window. The judge before whom he was taken for his court hearing happened to be the father of his fiancee! Even though this was greatly embarrassing, it may have proved to be his temporary salvation because the judge handled the case wisely and forced him into treatment rather than prison.

This young man's father also had died leaving a wife, a three-year-old girl, and a five-year-old son, the patient. He had not the faintest memory of his father, but he spoke of an almost utopian home life and family relationship in which all members were equal. This equality extended to the bathroom and to the bedrooms in that there was no thought of privacy in any part of the house at any time. He described a situation where all three, his mother, his sister, and he might be using the bathroom simultaneously for different purposes. If they were going out together, and togetherness was carried to an extreme in the family, they might shower and dress simultaneously. This seemed a perfectly normal and natural thing to him, and he denied ever having the faintest resemblance to sexual arousal from this close relationship, even though his sister was at the time he came into treatment a very attractive twenty-four-year-old unmarried girl. He not only denied experiencing sexual arousal, he appeared insulted that anyone could think of such a thing.

This young man's motivation for treatment rapidly vanished as soon as the court released the pressure upon him. He decided that he actually did not have a problem and that he "had learned his lesson" and that it would not happen again. Six months after he terminated psychiatric therapy, he was arrested for voyeurism and this time, coming before a different judge, he was given a heavy fine and six months in the county jail. This effectively shattered a promising career in geological engineering, and unless some miracle happens to motivate him into the proper treatment for a sufficient period of time, his condition is apt to recur upon release.

It is typical of the voyeur and of many other of the sexual deviates that they are unable to see the seriousness of the situation in which they put themselves. This young man quit treatment with the firm conviction that he would not succumb to the impulse again. He was a very intelligent person who was far above average in education and sophistication; yet he was able to ignore totally his own past history and the advice of many knowledgeable people. He was a criminal only in so far as he had broken the law, but six months in a county jail will have made a bitter and disillusioned person of him, and society will have lost a productive citizen.

Voyeurism has been discussed as if it referred exclusively to those who make nocturnal searches for windows through which to see the seminude or nude female. That type of activity is the most common, but some voyeurs prefer a less dangerous method. They find (or produce their own) holes in the walls of female public bathrooms and between the rooms of cheap hotels. Here they keep vigil until rewarded by a sight that sexually excites them. Many of these men may remain for hours at the chosen spot, and if "business" is good, as in a public place, they may have their own variety of an orgy!

Voyeurism does constitute an invasion of privacy, a valued commodity in our society, and as such it cannot be ignored. Neither the average citizen nor the police can determine with accuracy which man is a voyeur and which is a burglar about to enter a house; therefore, apprehension must be made. However, once it has been determined that the man is, in fact, a voyeur and not a man about to rob a house, legally enforced treatment makes far more sense than does imprisonment. It is neither humane nor reasonable, and it serves no useful function, to make a criminal of a man who is afflicted with a compulsive disorder he cannot control. Perhaps it is more logical to arrest a man with tuberculosis because he can be dangerous to those with whom he comes in contact.

The long-range goal of the study of all human dysfunctions is prevention. Some feel that today's feminine fashions are so revealing that the voyeur will no longer need to creep up to windows in hopes of seeing stimulating bits of female anatomy. This idea ignores the need of the voyeur to do his thing surreptitiously, and in all probability, the new freedom in exposure of the female anatomy will not affect voyeurism. Perhaps parental education would have a preventive effect. An understanding of the sexuality of childhood and some attention to the developing child's needs might do far more than punishment in adulthood. The core of prevention, as in many of the sexual disorders, is to furnish the growing child with identification models of the same sex, plus a healthy relationship to a figure of the opposite sex.

5

Pedophilia

Pedophilia (child molestation) is a condition in which a child is the preferred sexual object of an adult. The child molester (pedophile or pedophiliac) is universally abhorred and feared in modern Western society. The condition is far from rare and it has been known, but rarely accepted, in all cultures and all societies. Among the sexual deviations, it is second only to exhibitionism as a cause of arrest. Homosexual pedophilia, a condition in which a child of the same sex is the preferred object, is less common and is even more unacceptable in our culture. It may be termed a double sexual deviation (homosexuality plus pedophilia).

Children were not always so protected as they are in our culture. They were of considerable value as sexual objects in the Eastern countries prior to the eighteenth century. Even in Western societies little thought was given to the rights of children, and they were viewed as miniature adults on the one hand and as long term investments on the other. There were initially no laws or social standards for their benefit. Concern for children is a relatively modern affair.

Pedophilia is considered to be a condition afflicting only males. This is not entirely true, but reported cases of female pedophilia are so uncommon as to be of little significance. There is some evidence that the actual incidence may be greater than we think, but our society never becomes very excited by deviations in the sexual life of females. There are many reasons for this, but one is that the female is conceptualized as being sexually harmless, and despite modern evidence to the contrary, we still do not accept entirely the idea that a woman has active sexual impulses and drives. That she might seduce a helpless child into sexplay is unthinkable, and even if she did so, what harm can be done without a penis?

We will dismiss female pedophilia with this rather typical vignette:

During the course of psychiatric treatment a young male told of his frequent and intense sexual relations with his baby sitter over many years. He recalled that they began somewhere about his fifth or sixth year and that they continued almost until puberty. The sitter, a young, single female, was his constant companion for at least five days each week when he was not at school. Both his parents were professional people who were rarely at home, and he was an only child. His activities with the baby sitter consisted mainly of her playing with his penis and occasionally taking it into her mouth. Part of the "game" was her threatening to bite it off unless he were a "good" boy. Being a good boy including playing with her breasts and vagina, a task he came to enjoy immensely. She taught him to insert his penis into her vagina as he grew older, and this he enjoyed even more.

This behavior came to light during psychotherapy at age twenty, and it was never known to his parents. The child had become a young man with severe and deep-seated problems with his sexual identity, but the premature sexuality to which he was exposed may not have been the total cause of the difficulty, though it unquestionably played its part. It must be recalled that his parents were virtually absent from his childhood years, so that this neglect undoubtedly was equally important. It is difficult to evaluate the relative weight of these events, since parental supervision would have prevented the sexual exposures.

The point made here is that female pedophilia comes to light either long after the fact, or if it is detected earlier, it is lightly dismissed. The usual case consists of a baby sitter, maid, or female relative who, if caught, is either discharged or strongly reprimanded, and that is that! Most cases resemble pseudoaffairs in that they are apt to extend over some length of time, rather than to be one-time molestations. Unlike her male counterpart, the female pedophile is a great rarity in psychiatric practice or the police line-up, so knowledge of her is scanty.

The peak incidence of pedophilia occurs at three specific times in the life of the male: the teen ages, the mid-to-late thirties, and the mid-to-late fifties. There is nothing magical about these ages; they simply represent times of increased emotional stress during the male life span. Certainly there are many chronic pedophiles who manifest the condition continually from childhood to old age, and these ages of peak incidence may represent "getting caught" more than actual increased activity.

The psychopathology of pedophilia has many explanations, and it is probable that each of them is at least partially correct and that no single one covers all cases. All authorities agree that the condition can occur as a symptom in any form of severe mental disorder which reduces impulse control, or in any condition in which there is actual damage to the brain. However, we will be concerned with the condition as an entity unto itself and not as it might occur secondarily to some other derangement of mental functioning.

The condition is primarily a deviation in the choice of a sexual object. The pedophile does not see himself as a mature male, and although he may not be consciously aware of it, he does not feel sexually competent with the mature female. He may fantasize that the adult female would ridicule him for his lack of masculinity, so he does not place himself in this precarious position. He is so basically immature on the psychosexual level that he can only relate to an individual he believes to be in his own stage of emotional maturity. This level of psychosexual maturity is variable, and it may determine the age of the victim he chooses. Some men are singularly attracted to the very young, while others, the largest group, prefer those who are seven to ten years of age. Then there is a group which is attracted to prepubertal and pubertal females to the exclusion of all others. Nabokov's novel *Lolita* is a delightful account of this latter type of pedophilia.

The pedophile's background usually shows an inordinate attachment to and dependence upon the mother figure. The normal deep maternal attachment of the Oedipal period (ages four to six) appears to maintain itself throughout life. The father does not form an attractive object to which the son becomes attached, so that masculine identity, although not entirely absent, is faulty. Freud felt that the choice of a child as a sexual object represented a substitute for the mother, and that a more mature female would resemble a mother too closely for the man's comfort. The act can also represent the man treating a child as he wished (or wishes) to be treated by his mother. An element of both of these factors probably exists in most cases, but it must be remembered that all of this is in the unconscious of the pedophile and that he is not aware of either of these concepts. He tends to see himself as a normal but misunderstood person who prefers children to adults.

The sexual act of the pedophile rarely includes intercourse with the child. When this does occur, it frequently does not represent true pedophilia but rather is a symptom of a psychotic illness such as schizophrenia or of a damaged brain. The pedophile does not wish to harm the child, and genital intercourse occurs only in those whose preference is for the child in the "Lolita" age or one who is almost physically mature. Most frequently the pedophile merely wishes to caress the child or to have her caress or admire his genitalia or both. Occasionally he may wish to fondle the child's genital region while he masturbates, or he may attempt to get the child to stimulate him manually or to kiss his penis. An extremely small percentage attempt to insert a finger into the vagina, and even fewer (far less than 0.5 percent) may insert the penis between the little girl's thighs (intercrural intercourse).

The homosexual pedophile is more apt to encourage oral-genital contact, and it is generally assumed that he represents a more severe degree of psychosexual immaturity. Experience shows that treatment of this type of pedophilia is more difficult, more prolonged, and less frequently successful. Whereas heterosexual pedophilia usually is sporadic and may even be a one-time-only episode, this is the exception rather than the rule in homosexual pedophilia. Acts of violence also appear more frequently on the homosexual pedophile's record, but this seems logical in view of his greater degree of immaturity.

Parents frequently teach their little girls to be wary of strangers and to avoid being alone with unknown men. This may be good advice in general, but statistically it is of little value if protection of the child from sexual molestation is the object. The pedophile most frequently chooses as his sexual object either a member of his own family, such as a niece or a grandchild, or an associate of one of his relatives or friends. Frequently this is the playmate of his own children or grandchildren. The child will be well-known to him in almost three-fourths of the reported cases, and the place of sexual contact most frequently is the home of the child or of the molester. This makes an interesting contrast with the exhibitionist who, as previously stated, rarely exhibits himself except to total strangers and almost never to family members or associates.

The pedophile who chooses his own daughter will be

discussed in the chapter on incest. The behavioral motivations are those discussed plus the complicating force of living in close proximity and of already having an emotional tie to the child.

Let us illustrate many of the dynamic factors of pedophilia by an actual case history.

John came into psychiatric treatment directly from a prison sentence in which he had served five years for child molestation. He was thirty-nine years of age, and he previously had served a two-year sentence in his early teens for the same offense. He was an unmarried man who lived with his widowed mother in a small southwestern town. He had come to realize that he could not control his condition alone, and he knew a third sentence would be for life as an habitual criminal, so he literally begged for professional help. John's story was as follows:

He was the only child of a very hard-working, stern father and a very loving, but dependent and clinging mother. They were God-fearing people with definite fundamentalistic concepts of good and evil. John's earliest conscious memory of conflict with these concepts was in the first grade after he and another child (he could never be certain, but he thought it was a little girl) were discovered by a schoolteacher while comparing their genitalia. This was reported to John's parents who beat him "unmercifully" in order to teach him the evilness of his act. He recalled that such beatings were a fairly common consequence of any form of "bad" behavior, and that they were always administered by the father, but that he would be comforted by his mother after each of them. It came out in treatment that he was almost willing to pay the price of the beatings in order to obtain the seductive pacification which his mother was certain to offer afterward.

John could not recall ever having done anything right in his parents' opinion. He grew up with the idea that he was not competent as a son, a student, or as a male. He came to believe, as did the entire family, that sex was a concept wreathed in so much evil and filth that it should never be allowed into thoughts, let alone into words or actions, and yet he thought of it frequently. It was never mentioned in the house, and all John's factual knowledge came from his playmates and from the older boys who were always willing to be his sexual educators.

Although John recalled many playmates during his grammar school and high school years, there was never a very close chum, and there was never any form of a girl friend. His associates were more acquaintances than friends, and this probably because he was such a passive and obsequious person, always willing to do something for someone else and never making demands upon others. He stated that he was "too good" to be accepted by most groups and too shy to approach anyone alone.

John could not remember when his compulsive interest in little girls began. It was almost as if that first childhood experience at school, one certainly normal to that age, simply continued throughout life unabated. Although he was caught in sexual explorations several times during the early pubertal and adolescent years, all cases were settled by his parents and none became a legal question. Each time he was beaten severely by his father and restricted to the house for many days, but John always felt that this was perfectly justified. It was as if the beatings were acts of atonement which erased the previous act and allowed him to start all over again.

He could recall only one period of freedom from the pedophiliac impulse in his entire life, and that was during the three years he spent in the army. He recalls that he thought about it frequently when he was a soldier, but that he was able to control it easily. Throughout all of his post-pubertal years he resorted to frequent masturbation, and upon a few occasions he was able to have heterosexual intercourse with a paid prostitute. He had an occasional date with a woman, but he managed to avoid sexual contact. This was not always easy because women thought John appealing and often made advances, which he found flattering but which made him uncomfortable and apprehensive.

John's "modus operandi" in adulthood was to find a small girl on the street or in a park, usually one about five to eight years of age, who attracted him. He would arrange to bump into her in some relatively secluded spot or to entice her into his automobile. He would speak to her of "little girl things" and perhaps give her candy or chewing gum. He would manage to fondle her, usually on her thighs and buttocks, and eventually he would ask her to look at his penis. If her reaction was good; that is, if she did not appear too frightened or if she showed curiosity, he would ask her to touch his penis. Never had he gone beyond that nor had he ever attempted sexual intercourse with the children. He did not understand how anyone could possibly suspect him of such a dastardly act, and he had only contempt and hatred for any man who would do such a thing.

John rationalized his behavior in a manner common to many pedophiles. He was a great supporter of sexual education, and he blamed much of his own problem on the lack of it in his youth. He stated that his relationship with a little girl provided her with a method of learning about sex from a kind and understanding adult who would not shame or condemn her. He elaborated upon his love for children and his concern for their future in such a manner as to insinuate that he should be allowed his activities freely for the benefit of little girls!

John's personality was rather typical for that of the average pedophile. He was ill at ease among men, but he wanted greatly to be accepted by them. He liked everyone, but he was unsure as to how people felt about him. He was always an underachiever since he did not conceptualize himself as being able to compete on an equal basis with his peers. He was scrupulously honest and would go to any lengths to avoid hurting the feelings of others. He rarely felt open anger and never antagonized anyone deliberately. In short, with the exception of his deviate sexual practice, John was an ideal citizen who had never been in any other trouble, not even in traffic court. Parenthetically, John received a full pardon from the governor after two years of group psychotherapy, and a man who might otherwise have spent his life in prison is now a good and productive citizen operating his own small business.

The victim of the pedophile frequently is believed to have suffered physical damage and irreparable psychic trauma. She may be rushed to a doctor's office where she is given a minute examination which may include smears to see if any sperm can be identified in the vagina. There is a great deal of fear and hysteria in the family, and the police are excited and vengeful. The neighborhood is up in arms, and in short, it is communicated to the child that something horrible must have happened to her. This may come as a complete surprise to the child who may have been bored or disgusted by her contact, but more likely than not found it rather amusing and exciting. The sexual curiosity of a child and her willingness to cooperate with anyone who encourages it should never be underestimated.

It is the parental overreaction, legal excitement, and medical manipulation that may harm the child. The forced physical examination rarely is necessary and should be avoided unless there is evidence that some form of violence actually has occurred. This will be very rare, and when it has happened, it will be quite obvious in a little girl, and it will not necessitate a minute examination to detect it. Hysteria and excitement should be avoided if at all possible, and the incident should be handled simply as an unfortunate contact with a disturbed individual. Court appearances, testimonies, and cross-examination should be avoided at all costs.

The parents should act as if no great thing has occurred, but they should make themselves available for the child's questions, which should be answered calmly and truthfully but without elaboration. They should understand that no harm actually has happened in more than 99 percent of the cases. It is essential to inform the police in most states, but again, this should be done cooly and calmly. When all is handled in this matter-of-fact way, there is no evidence that one need worry about the damaging effects of the act upon the child.

This child's cooperation and curiosity deserve further mention. Freud forever laid to rest the concept that a child is totally devoid of sexual interest and feeling. Some children exhibit this interest quite overtly and in a straight-forward manner whenever the opportunity is available. Others are far more inhibited and restrained in their expression of sexuality. The seductiveness of a young girl may appear cute and innocent to the average male, but to a man who already finds them sexually attractive and whose impulse control is weak, this seductive behavior may be overwhelming, as the following vignette illustrates:

An electrician was called to make some repairs in a suburban home. The mother asked if her six-year-old girl would be bothersome if she remained at home while the mother went grocery shopping. The workman assured her that it would present no problem and that he was very fond of little girls.

Shortly after the mother left the home, the little girl squatted by the electrician, pulled down her panties and asked him if he had something like she had. The mother, who had forgotten her purse, returned for it just in time to see the man caressing the nude genital region of her daughter. The police were called and the man was taken to jail.

This man was fifty-five years of age. He readily confessed to the consulting psychiatrist to whom the court referred him that he had been attracted to young girls all his life, but he adamantly insisted that he had never succumbed to the temptation before this time, and certainly he had no police record. The direct, suggestive behavior of the six-year-old girl had shattered his resistance and the latent condition had broken into reality. Perhaps his resistance was already weakened because it soon became evident that he was depressed over the recent discovery that his wife was ill with an incurable disease.

The role of the little girl as an active participant in pedophilia has received considerable attention from those interested in human behavior. The greatest number of the victims are between six and eight years of age, a time where there is considerable sexual curiosity. They not only make willing victims, they actually may initiate the sexual play with an adult who appears receptive to them. They tend to come from homes in which questions about, or even allusions to, sexually or genital anatomy have been severely discouraged. The suppression of their normal curiosity has not weakened its force nor destroyed it. It merely awaits the proper moment for reemergence.

Another factor that has been noted with undue frequency in these little girls is their seductive behavior toward adults. Investigations have shown that they come from homes in which they have received less affection and care than they needed. Their seductive behavior appears to be a search for the love and attention their environment has not given them. The man willing to give this to them may find himself tempted beyond his ability to control his immature impulses.

Most cases come to legal or medical attention by accident. The man is surprised in the act, as in the case of the electrician, or the little girl inadvertently and innocently tells of her friendship and play. It is rare that the girl reports the incident (or incidents) with an idea that something is amiss, and it is even rarer for physical damage to the child to be the cause of the man's apprehension.

The elderly man arrested for pedophilia needs special mention. The senile changes of aging, combined with the loss of self-esteem that frequently comes with forced retirement and old age, may produce regression in the man. He may see himself as becoming childlike and dependent in many ways, but one of the earliest manifestations of this may be in the sexual sphere. His failing mental and physical powers, including sexual powers, may lead him to approach a child in a seductive manner simply because he unconsciously perceives himself to be the same age on an emotional level. He usually becomes friends with the child with no thought of overt sexuality, and he may be more shocked than anyone else when he finds himself so deeply involved.

The disgrace of arrest and the attendant publicity frequently plunges these elderly men into a suicidal depression. Compassion and understanding is never needed more than with these unfortunate victims of aging. Fortunately, unlike the younger chronic pedophile, the elderly male is not apt to repeat the act once he has suffered the shock and embarrassment of detection.

An elderly male in a neighboring apartment volunteered to sit with a five-year-old girl while her mother went shopping. This became an almost daily event enjoyed by all since the mother welcomed a chance to get away without the expense of a sitter. The man needed something to do; and the little child became genuinely fond of her new and attractive friend.

A neighbor informed the mother that she had seen the old man doing something indecent to the child. A trap was laid so that the mother surprised her daughter and the elderly sitter with the man's hand on the little girl's nude genitals. The kindly old man of yesterday suddenly became an evil sex fiend who was arrested and jailed immediately. The physician at the jail recognized that the man was in severe congestive heart failure and rightfully had him transferred to the hospital. His brain, already aging, was being embarrassed further by the lack of oxygen secondary to the heart condition. Both the outraged mother and the police responded to reason and the charges were dropped.

The pedophile should be given psychiatric consultation and, with the exception of the senile man, he usually will warrant long-term treatment. Jail sentences are of no value to an individual who has succumbed to impulses beyond his control. In fact, imprisonment is harmful in that it further undermines his already failing self-esteem and makes him more likely to repeat the act. The pedophile is treated as the lowest form of existence in the prison culture. The other prisoners hold him in extreme disgust and make his life a constant misery. They appear to focus all their frustrations and pent-up hostilities upon him, and since he is a passive man by nature, he is unable to defend himself. The other prisoners quickly learn that he can be used, and they take full advantage of this and frequently make him the object of homosexual and sadistic practices. If he resists, a few "sessions" with his prison mates will convince him to cooperate.

This era of sexual enlightenment fortunately is bringing with it a more humane and understanding attitude toward these benighted men. Treatment may not always be successful, especially in homosexual pedophilia, but without question psychiatric evaluation is indicated in each case. Group psychotherapy is an effective and efficient treatment method in the proper setting and when run by competent people. It is available in most larger communities and in many institutions. If the evaluation shows more severe mental pathology such as a psychosis, mental retardation, or pedophilia associated with a sadistic element, then appropriate treatment, including confinement when indicated, can be recommended. Imprisonment without proper treatment is not only wasteful of public money, it is inhuman and irrational.

6

Transvestism

TRANSVESTISM (CROSS DRESSING) is a condition in which sexual excitement or gratification is derived from dressing in the clothing of the opposite sex. There is an obvious relationship between this condition and fetishism (discussed in chapter eight), and this is especially true in those cases in which the transvestite male uses only a single, and usually hidden, female garment. There remain some critical differences between transvestism and fetishism, and one is that the fetishist does not wish to be seen by others, whereas the transvestite prefers either to parade his activity before others or to admire himself in a mirror. Other differences will become clear in the chapter on fetishism.

Transvestism apparently occurs in some form in most cultures and has been known for centuries. Herodotus, the magnificent, if somewhat overimaginative Greek historian of the pre-Christian era, wrote about the Scythians who lived on the shores of the Black Sea. He was amazed to find that some of the men not only wore female clothing frequently but that they also engaged in activities traditionally reserved for females. Herodotus explained this peculiar behavior as being one method by which the goddess Aphrodite had punished the Scythians because they had once plundered her temple. The fact that Herodotus spoke in terms of punishment undoubtedly means that the condition was considered abnormal and undesirable by the Greeks of that era.

Hippocrates, who wrote of almost everything involving human beings, included transvestism among his observations. He apparently originated an etiological theory about the cause of transvestism that continued for over two thousand years without question or correction. He theorized that transvestism occurred when too much horseback riding had produced an atrophy of the testicles and a lack of manliness! This theory must have come naturally from his observations of the feminine characteristics of castrated men, but he was wrong in connecting it with either horseback riding or castration. Neither Herodotus nor Hippocrates mentioned female transvestism, but the etiological theory of Hippocrates would have been sorely tested had he done so!

Forms of transvestism have occurred within recent centuries in a stylized form in at least two American Indian tribes. The "Mujerado" of the Pueblo Indians was a transvestite male who was used as a homosexual object in certain religious festivals upon rare occasions. The Mujerado was supposed to ride horses and to masturbate, somewhat in keeping with the theory purported by Hippocrates, in order to remain feminine. Another Indian group from the Plains allowed the male transvestites, called "Berdache," to be valued members of the social group and to function as pediatricians, but they could not hope to obtain tribal honors or hold positions of power among the men. Their social positions and tribal aspirations could not exceed that of the female.

Transvestism does occur in both sexes, although it appears to be much more common in males. The fact that the female may dress in male clothing without attracting attention or derogation may account for most of this apparent difference today, although this freedom did not always exist and could not account for the condition in earlier days. The much greater freedom allowed the modern woman in choosing her clothing also provides a more available outlet for those cases of borderline psychopathology. The key, however, is whether or not the individual cross dresses as sexual stimulation or as a prelude to it, and it appears that the female does not do so. There are no reported cases of females who require masculine clothing before they can function in a normal heterosexual manner nor are there reports of females who use male dress to arouse them to a near orgastic level. Most women who appear to be female transvestites are actually homosexuals of the "butch" type who prefer to look as masculine as possible.

The cause of transvestism, as with most of the sexual deviations, stems from the very early phases of psychosexual development. The psychoanalytical theory is that transvestism is an attempt to overcome the fear of castration by creating an imaginary woman with a penis and subsequently identifying with her. In other words, by dressing as a woman and either looking at himself in a mirror or having someone else look at him and compliment him, the man identifies as a woman. Since he has a strong, unconscious feeling that only the woman has a penis that can be used, he thereby achieves his own fantasied masculinity and continues to function, more or less, as a male.

A practitioner of transvestism can preserve his fantasies of a dual existence. He becomes the admired woman who has both strength and beauty; then, following this experience, he becomes a sexually potent male. The tragedy is that these roles are based on pathology, and as a result, he never becomes very good at either one. He is doomed to a shadowy in-between sexual life.

Probably not every male transvestite develops his warped sexuality through the same mechanism. An excellent study published by Dr. Robert J. Stoller showed that it was almost always a significant female, usually the mother, who started the male in the cross-dressing role. He found that these women could be divided into three categories: the malicious male haters, the supporters (succorers), and the symbiotes.

The first group, the malicious male haters, was all that the name implies. Since the son rapidly learned that mother hated all males, he readily assumed a nonmale role in order to escape his mother's hatred. He learned that mother approved of him only when he dressed and acted as if he were female, and he, like every child, wanted his mother's approval. He did not develop a true female identification such as might have produced transsexualism, however, probably because his mother made a very unattractive female role model, and so he learned to sit somewhere on the fence!

The second group of mother, the succorers, was more feminine than the first group and was not so openly competitive and scornful of the male. They had the fear of masculinity and the need to downgrade it that is so common to all of these women, but they did not actually hate males. Like the men haters, they enjoyed seeing males dressed as females and encouraged their sons to do so. This type of woman appears to gain a feeling of power from knowing that she controls the male by making him into a sham female. She can retain her own power only by "feeding," as it were, off the male.

The third group, the symbiotes, was composed of women who were strongly bisexual in nature. They spontaneously and compellingly drove their sons to dress in female clothing as if it were a perfectly natural thing to do. They were hostile to all males except their sons who were becoming feminized and were seen not so much as individuals in their own right, but as appendages inseparable from their mothers. These mothers kept their sons in a symbiotic (pathologically close) relationships so that the sons could never develop ego boundaries that could be perceived as separate from that of the mother's body. They dressed as she dressed simply because they saw themselves as a part of the maternal body.

One can readily become convinced that the female is the culprit in all phases of human sexual maldevelopment unless one keeps in mind that the father figure also plays an important role, even if only by his absence. For the sort of thing we have been discussing to occur requires that the man of the family allow it either passively or actively. The father either does not produce an adequate figure of masculinity for his little boy, or he produces the figure, but makes it so unattractive that the son turns back toward the seductive female in self-defense. It is probable that no mother could produce a transvestite without either the permission or the total absence of the father. By and large, this statement will hold true for most of the sexual deviations and even of the nondeviant sexual problems of males.

Very little is written about the etiology of the female transvestite. It appears that she is the product of a reverse situation in that she perceives all of the important attributes of living to stem from masculinity. She desires a penis at some level of consciousness, not necessarily because of the sexual connotations, but because it stands symbolically for the male freedom and prowess traditionally denied the female. She may capture the fantasies and feelings of having the male prerogatives by dressing herself in the form of the one who traditionally possesses the penis. Again, it probably requires that both parents give the girl the impression that being feminine is of little value and that maleness is all important. The normal attraction of a little girl to her father gives him a strong position in this development period. In order to produce a female who feels proud of her role and wants to pretain it, the father must show that being female will warrant masculine approval, in this case his approval. Both parents must transmit to the girl that femininity produces positive rewards in adulthood.

Transvestism takes many forms and frequently blends into other types of deviations. Some transvestites are homosexual, some are bisexual, and perhaps even more of them are heterosexual. The heterosexual drive is rarely as great as seen in the average male if one uses frequency of intercourse as a barometer, and many investigators believe that this is partly because of the strong narcissistic component so frequently found. The confirmed transvestite needs either to admire himself in a mirror while dressed in female clothing or to be seen and admired by another, preferrably a woman. The core of much of his behavior is his own self-love—a love so strong that little is available for a woman. In some instances he can function quite well as a heterosexual male only after admiring himself or being admired, but in others he may prefer masturbation or no sexual activity at all, although masturbation is apt to be the main sexual activity.

Mr. Vail, a junior executive in the television industry, exemplified the male transvestite who could function heterosexually only after being admired in female attire. He was seen in psychiatric consultation for a moderate depression at the age of thirty-eight. He had been married for fourteen years and had three children, ages five, seven, and eleven. His wife was an attractive woman, somewhat masculine in appearance, who found his condition amusing but of little concern, and she was willing and able to cooperate with him in his habit. She was reluctant to discuss it since she did not see a connection between it and her husband's depression.

Mr. Vail's parents were not available for interview, but he recalled vividly that his mother was a "man hater." His father had deserted them when he was approximately four years of age, and he had heard nothing good said about either his father, or men in general, afterward. He felt in retrospect that perhaps his mother also hated him, because the favorite punishment of his mother, and of an aunt who came to live with them, was to dress him in female clothing and to make fun of him simultaneously. Sometimes they would invite visitors and even his playmates to observe him in his predicament. To dress in female clothing ceased to be a punishment and became a pleasure as he grew older, and with this change in his own feelings came a change in mother's attitude. She began to praise him and to admire him rather than to berate and tease him. The young Mr. Vail had followed the old adage, "If you can't whip them, join them."

The young man's early school years were practically wiped from his memory. These were the times when he was being subjected to the mortification of parading before other children in his female clothes. Almost every other memory was pleasant, but there were very few of them. It was as if he had no desire to recall any of that period that could be repressed.

Mr. Vail had not dated until his last year of high school and then only in a very platonic manner. He married the first woman he ever dated with any degree of seriousness because he admired her strength of character and her apparent goodness. There was no sexual contact beyond kissing until after marriage. Mr. Vail found that the practice he had used as a prelude to masturbation since puberty now had to be continued before intercourse in marriage. This was to dress in female stockings, panties, and brassière and to apply violent red lipstick. He would gaze with unabashed admiration at his reflection in the mirror, then masturbate. After marriage he preferred to have his wife admire him and verbally make commendatory statements about his good looks. (Mrs. Vail had assumed the role previously filled by his mother.) He could then remove the lipstick and the female clothing and be heterosexually active. He was virtually impotent without this practice, and he continued to masturbate one or two times weekly despite frequent intercourse with his wife.

Mr. Vail looked and acted much like another male approaching middle age. He was an active member of the American Legion and was quite proud of his good record in the military. He, like most male transvestites, was a relatively quiet and unassuming man who was looked upon as a good neighbor and as a model citizen. His neighborhood associates and those who worked for him and with him would have been unutterably shocked to know that they had a sexual deviant in their midst!

Morris represents a slightly more pathological version of transvestism. He was seen in psychiatric consultation at the request of the police department after he had been arrested while walking in the park clad in a complete outfit of female clothing and wearing a platinum blonde wig. He apparently made a very pathetic figure of a woman and his stubble of dark beard and his hairy legs had combined with his awkward gait to attract the attention of a policeman. Morris was promptly arrested for impersonating a woman—an act that is a crime in many states despite its apparent harmlessness.

Morris was an unmarried veteran of World War II who had been arrested while "celebrating" his fortieth birthday. He lived alone in a modest apartment and, while he had some few acquaintances with whom he could visit and play cards, he had no real friends. Life had been very lonely and difficult for Morris since the death of his mother approximately five years previously. He had been an only child, and he could not recall anything about his father except that his mother had always refused to talk about him. He had developed the fantasy that his mother had not been married at all, and that he was illegitimate. He saw his mother as the sweet, innocent girl betrayed by a villainous man who had misled her with promises of marriage.

Morris recalled his mother as being "angelic," a woman without fault. He did not appear to resent the fact that she had encouraged him to develop feminine traits and that she had dressed him in female garments from a very early age. She continued to help him choose the female clothing, of which he had an extensive wardrobe, until the time of her death. Since they had lived together for over thirty-five years, the routine had evolved for Morris to dress in female clothing two or three times per week after dinner. Mother would compliment him and admire him greatly as he walked about the house. Then they would watch television together, frequently holding hands, until bedtime. Morris would gaze fondly at himself in his female attire in a full length mirror before taking off the clothes preparatory to getting ready for bed. He would get an erection while doing this, and he invariably masturbated. He adamantly denied any particular masturbatory fantasies.

Morris had not been away from his mother a single night prior to his induction into the army at age nineteen. He was discharged because of a neurotic condition after about eight months, most of which he spent either on sick call or in the hospital awaiting discharge. His brief military career had been the most unpleasant time of his life. He had found the sexual banter of barrack's life vulgar and disgusting and his fellow soldiers crude and undesirable. Of course, he had not been accepted by his peers who rode him unmercifully about his mother fixation and his "sissiness."

The relationship between Morris and his mother was definitely the symbiotic type described by Stoller. The bonds between mother and son had been separable only by death, and even then, Morris remained emotionally bound to her. Morris' life had consisted only of his work in a local department store and of his mother. Although they attended church and some few civic functions together, they took no real part in the community. They had only themselves, and once the mother was gone, Morris was alone. A life that had always been empty and unhappy by normal standards now become a miserable one.

It appeared amazing that Morris had been able to function even marginally for the five years since his mother's death before "arranging" his arrest. His arrest had occurred on the first and only time that Morris had gone out of the house in his female garb. It was very difficult to believe that he had not desired, unconsciously of course, to be arrested. Certainly, it was obvious to any observer that he was not a woman, and he must have sensed that walking through the park in the middle of the day was going to attract attention and apprehension in the town where he lived.

The developmental stages of Morris' life were so completely devoid of normal masculine identification figures that Morris had no chance of becoming a man. It was not surprising that he had developed into a withdrawn, retiring person unable to exist without his mother, but rather it was remarkable that he had been able to exist even marginally for so long. His arrest led to psychiatric care, but Morris had no motivation for change and no desire to enter the world of men. He simply gave up, and when last known, he was in a domicile unit of the Veterans Administration.

Some authorities feel that transvestism differs from transsexualism only in degree. There is a major difference, however, and this difference is readily discernible. The transsexual, both consciously and unconsciously, desires to be physically what he is mentally—a woman. If he dresses in female clothing, he does so in keeping with the general emotional identification he truly feels. The transvestite, on the other hand, dresses in female clothing not only to be a mock female but to make himself feel more masculine! Therein lies the major difference between the two conditions. The transsexual only wants to be fully a female, but the transvestite, wanting to be more masculine but perceiving the female to be the true holder of masculine organs, must first detour through this devious identification route. The transsexual would like to lose his penis and scrotum, but the thought of this would horrify a true transvestite as much as the average heterosexual male.

Even Morris, who consciously appeared to detest masculinity, had his unconscious desires to be manly. On a conscious level, he had long since given up any hope of achieving male independence from mother, and by the time she died, it was too late.

For a male to wear female clothing in public is a criminal offense punishable by law in many states. It does not receive a great deal of attention, and in most large cities it is considered a nuisance rather than a real social danger. This is as it should be; in fact, it should not be against the law at all. The condition indicates psychopathology, but it is a type that is purely personal and should be of no concern to legal agencies since it is of no social significance. The laws against transvestism were passed not because of the sexual aspects of the condition, but with the idea of preventing crime by men in female disguise. The laws were passed back in the days when women wore long dresses and face-hiding bonnets—a far cry from modern styles.

Sometimes the transvestite finds himself in embarrassing situations or becomes so uncomfortable about his own feelings of inadequacy and immaturity that he seeks psychiatric treatment. This does not happen very frequently, but when it does, psychoanalytically oriented psychotherapy or group therapy is the treatment of choice. More often, the condition is ego-syntonic (does not produce anxiety of any type) and remains unnoticed unless it comes to light accidentally or in the course of a psychiatric history. The propensity of the transvestite to develop depression or intense anxiety frequently leads him to psychiatric care.

Prevention must occur in early childhood—the early childhood of the future parent! Only a parent with a fair degree of satisfaction in his own sexual role can transmit this satisfaction to the child, and this goes for both sexes. Obviously, dressing a child in the clothing of the opposite sex, either as punishment or as a sign of dissatisfaction with the child's gender, should be avoided at all times. The mother who desires a female child and who is disappointed in producing a male must come to realize that the boy can only become, at best, a ludicrous caricature of a girl and a warped, inadequate male.

7

Transsexualism

TRANSSEXUALISM IS A condition in which an individual possesses the chromosomes, anatomy, and the physiology of one sex, but the mind and psyche of the opposite sex. This distinct split between the morphological and the psychological sex is thought by some to represent a more advanced stage of the condition discussed in the preceding chapter on transvestism. However, there are marked differences in both degree and quality in that the transvestite does not question his core gender (male or female), and he does not wish to have it changed. He certainly has no desire to have his genitalia mutilated. The transsexual male feels himself to be a woman trapped in a man's body, and he views his external genitalia with hatred and disgust, or as one such individual stated, "as ugly tumors" growing on the body. He may go to great difficulty and submit to painful expensive procedures to remove these "tumors." Some, in either desperation or due to psychotic breaks, have amputated their own genitalia when refused surgery.

Christine Jorgensen is the most famous example of male transsexualism. The publicity given this case prompted many others to come forward seeking the type of surgical transformation that apparently turned a very unhappy male into a reasonably contented and successful woman. Hundreds of conversion operations have been performed in this country and abroad during the ensuing twenty years, although this type of operation is relatively new in the United States. Attempts at other forms of therapy, designed either to make the transsexual person happy with his situation or to convert him to normal heterosexuality have not been as successful.

The etiology of transsexualism is debatable and may be compounded of multiple facets. Genetic and endocrine causes have been discussed and researched, but there simply is no scentific evidence to support these theories. Psychological causes are far more probable, and as was discussed in chapter one, imprinting or some form of a childhood conditioning are now generally accepted in all theories of etiology. These are difficult concepts to prove with hard scientific validity, but both animal experiments and human histories support them. Unfortunately, these causative events occur before the patient is old enough to remember them, and we must rely upon third party information, usually from parents or relatives. Human experimentation to confirm or deny the work that has been done on animals is out of the question, but nature has provided us with a living laboratory in the many individuals born with ambiguous or with totally misleading genitalia. These unfortunate people frequently are of one chromosomal and endocrinological sex, but are mistakenly raised as the opposite sex. Almost without exception, they identify as the sex assigned to them for the first two and one-half years of life. It appears virtually impossible to reverse the situation after that age. This leads us to believe that perfectly normal children could grow to adulthood with the inner sense of one sex, but with the body of the other.

Transsexualism is not just a degree of homosexuality. The difference is rather obvious when the overt homosexual male is asked how he would feel about having his penis removed. Most will react as quickly and as negatively as heterosexual men. It is true that transsexual males may date men and fall in love with them, but *they do so as if they were females,* and that is an important distinction to make. Their emotional investment is heterosexual in nature, and their erotic desires are consistent with this.

Some transsexual men have functioned in a normal marital relationship, and many have reported successful sexual relationships with women. One method of achieving this is illustrated by a thirty-year-old man who had fathered two children. Heterosexual intercourse was possible only when the woman assumed the superior position during the sexual act; then the man imagined that the penis belonged to the woman and was inserted into him. In fantasy he became the female of the sexual partnership and was able to function to orgasm.

Transsexualism is a disturbance in the core gender as was illustrated by the case of Miss Johnson in chapter one. This type of female transsexualism appears to be much rarer than the male variety, but this could be more apparent than real because the male is seen more frequently in medical practice due to the far greater possibility of corrective surgery. The female has the advantage of being more socially acceptable when acting a male role than does a man in the reverse situation. While it is as yet not possible to transform a normal female body into a functioning male, the opposite can be done with relative ease and success. Amputation of the penis and scrotum and the formation of a workable vagina is readily done, but grafting on or manufacturing a functional penis for the female body is another story. Attempts have been made to do this by some bold and innovative surgeons, but the results have not yet justified the work and the risks. The following case is illustrative of male transsexualism.

Bob first came for medical help when he was twenty-four years of age. He wrote from a town about five hundred miles away and stated that he would come for an interview if any possibility of transformation existed. His letter stated,

"I am true female," and "I am woman doomed to a miserable life in a male body." It was a well-written letter with nothing to make one think of mental illness. He had read of the surgical procedure in a lay magazine, and for the first time, he felt that life held some promise for him. He said, "Life is not worth living unless I can be a woman as was intended."

Bob appeared for the interview dressed appropriately and neatly in a business suit, shirt, and conservative tie. The only possibility of distinguishing him from a normal young businessman or one of our medical students was his overly long and beautifully coiffed hair (long hair on males was not common in his area) and his carefully manicured and lacquered fingernails. There were none of the caricatured feminine mannerisms sometimes seen in overt homosexuals, and his voice and speech intonations, although not overly masculine, were certainly within normal limits. Even though he did not look or act feminine, the interviewer soon felt that he was relating to a woman.

Bob had been born in a small southwestern town while his father was on military duty early in World War II. The father returned when Bob was less than three years of age and promptly left his wife and was never seen or heard from again. Bob and his mother, now a woman thoroughly embittered toward men, lived a rather isolated life with virtually no outside contacts except the maternal grandmother who visited about once monthly. Not a single male identification figure existed in his developmental years. His mother later told him that she had always wanted a girl and that she had dressed him entirely in female clothing until he started school at age six. A picture had been made of him just before he received his male clothing and a haircut (his first one), and it showed for all purposes a perfectly normal and attractive young girl with long, dark hair. He continued to wear female clothing when alone with his mother or when playing by himself until he finished high school.

School furnished Bob his first contact with peers. He

felt uncomfortable with boys, and he found their rough and tumble games not to his liking. Their sexualized talk and jokes embarrassed him to tears. He much preferred to play house and dolls with girls. With his mother's encouragement, he was able to associate with a peer group almost exclusively female.

Bob slept in the same bed with his mother every night of his life until he left home to attend beauty college at the age of eighteen. He recalled no feelings of sexual stimulation, but he did remember the many pleasant winter evenings of cuddling under the blankets with mother. His early years, drab and lonely by average standards, were recalled as pleasant and secure with just the two of them in a small house on the edge of a small western town. He recalled that it would have been idyllic had it not been for the teasing and ridicule he received from the other boys his age. He was always referred to as "sissy," and he was drubbed many times by these male peers, but he never fought back despite the fact that he was large for his age. His many bruises and bloody noses were soothed by a loving mother who used these incidents to point out to Bob the depravity of males and the undesirability of being one.

It is worth interrupting Bob's story a moment to draw attention to the similarity between his background and that of many male transvestites. It may well be that only a subtle difference due to some accident of development decides whether or not the child becomes a transsexual or a transvestite.

Bob recalled no overt sexual feelings one way or the other during the postpubertal and early adolescent years. Physiological puberty apparently occurred at a normal age, but either he repressed all memory of early adolescent sexuality, or it simply was not there. He recalled his first masturbation to orgasm at about sixteen or seventeen during which he fantasized himself as female. He learned to precede the occasional masturbatory acts by tucking his penis between his compressed thighs, standing in front of a mirror and fantasizing that he was a female. The sight of his own penis was revolting to him, and he never was comfortable while urinating unless he was sitting like a female. Urination in public places such as bus stations and school latrines always presented a problem, and he avoided it when possible. He flatly refused to dress in the same room with boys during compulsory gym class at high school. Somehow his mother wangled a medical excuse and saved him from suspension from classes.

Bob became a fairly successful beautician in a large southwestern city, and mother moved in with him. He related well to his female customers as one girl to another, but he felt no sexual attraction toward any of them. Neither was he attracted sexually to males, although he had frequent fantasies of being loved by a man and of becoming a housewife and mother. He appeared to have very little sex drive, and he had ceased his occasional masturbation by age twenty. He stated that the very process of masturbation and ejaculation, while it gave him a pleasant feeling, was disgusting and repulsive to him. It appeared as if the touch of his own penis reminded him of the unpleasant but inescapable fact that he was physically a male.

Psychiatric interviews and psychological tests revealed that Bob was a rather shy, aloof, passive individual with a self-identity predominantly female. There were hysterical features to his personality, and projective tests revealed great body consciousness. He showed some antisocial personality traits, but there was no element of flagrant psychopathology except for his confused gender role and a tendency toward depression. His full scale IQ was slightly above average (108), and his verbal ability was somewhat higher than his performance scores. There apeared to be no contraindication to surgery on the basis of either the interviews or the psychological testing.

All of the possible dangers and postoperative difficulties,

both social and physical, of a surgical change were explained to Bob in detail. No attempt was made to encourage him to continue his search for conversion surgery. Nothing appeared to shake his motivation for surgery; in fact, he stated that life was not worth living without the hope of being transformed. He was willing to settle for amputation of the penis and scrotum, although he preferred to become a complete woman with a functioning vagina. He had several hundred dollars saved toward the medical and hospital bills, and he planned to return to work as a beautician as soon as possible. His mother did not understand the procedure entirely, but she was pleased by the prospect of trading a son for a daughter and proceeded to do what she could toward financing it.

It was decided that Bob could receive the proper treatment much nearer to his job, and a referral was made to a local clinic interested in transsexualism. He received six months of estrogenic therapy to suppress his gonadal function and to start breast development. During this period he began a long process of electrolysis for a rather dark and noticeable beard, and he began seeing a psychiatrist once weekly. He did not waver in his desire for surgery, and this was performed approximately seven and one-half months after Bob first sought consultation. He received the full treatment with the creation of an artificial vagina, and at the last contact *she* was dating a young man with whom she was having occasional sexual intercourse with pleasure and excitement, but as yet without orgasm. Bob had become Roberta, and on first report, she was happy in her new life.

Her major postoperative difficulties were not with the surgery, as this went smoothly and pleased her highly, but with the many bits of bureaucratic red tape, such as birth certificate, driver's license, draft card, and social security registration. The problems here are almost unimaginable, and they clearly stem from a legal stance that is emotional rather than logical.

Not all transsexuals have histories so blatantly abnormal. Many do have fathers and come from a home life not far from normal, at least on the surface. Many have had normal siblings. Even the closest study does not always give an answer as to why the deviation occurred. It has been suggested, but not substantiated, that some gene on a sex chromosome determines the sense of core gender. This would make possible an abnormality in which the female gene becomes attached to the male chromosome (Y) and produces a chromosomal male (XY) with a female core gender. The female transsexual would be a chromosomal female (XX) with the male gene attached to one of the X chromosomes.

Some medical, legal, and religious authorities, many more a few years ago than at present, have condemned the conversion operations bitterly. They have stated that transsexualism is emotional in origin and that an emotional disturbance should be treated by psychological means, that is, by psychotherapy. Others base their objections on a moral belief that it is "sinful" to tamper with nature. The plain truth is that psychotherapeutic measures have failed, and it appears more sinful to sentence an individual to a life of unhappiness than to "tamper with nature" and produce a happy person. The vast majority of transsexual men are not interested in psychotherapy and will not cooperate with, much less pay for, long years of psychoanalysis even if it were guaranteed successful. Dr. Harry Benjamin, one of the world's true experts on transsexualism, once stated that he had never heard of a cure by psychotherapy in spite of the fact that some patients had been in psychoanalytic treatment for over three years.

The conversion operation is the wish of most transsexuals. It is extremely important that the physician be certain that this wish is a permanent conviction in a relatively mature individual. It may seem like a contradiction to speak of maturity in these people, but many of them are relatively mature in all realms of their personality except that of sexual identity. This can be determined by psychiatric interviews, psychological tests, and by several months of observation during which estrogen therapy is given as a sort of reversible chemical castration. It is extremely important that the patient receive a psychiatric consultation so that the surgeon may be assured of the patient's competency to make this drastic decision and may be further assured that no psychosis, even of a borderline nature, exists. Occasional schizophrenic men try to get themselves operated upon, and failing this, may resort to self-mutilation.

Many transsexuals show a variety of personality disorders bordering on the antisocial. The general instability is not unlike that seen with many of the sexual abnormalities. Sexual identity is a very basic aspect of personality structure, so basic that it is almost inconceivable that it be greatly awry with the other parts of the personality unblemished. This aspect of some transsexuals makes them difficult patients to work with, and it adds to the resistances of those who do not wish the operation to become commonplace.

It is relatively important to be certain that a successful woman can be produced by the surgical process before taking the first major step. This may mean that other forms of plastic surgery are essential, for example, the removal of an overly large thyroid cartilege or the repair of a broken nose. Some male faces simply do not lend themselves to femaleness without extensive reworking, and others are totally impossible. A gawky man of six feet and four inches with a hatchet face and protruding ears might make a relatively poor and unhappy woman! All of these factors must be considered and discussed with the patient before surgery is started.

The surgical conversion consists of the removal of the scrotum and the penis and the fashioning of an artificial vagina between the anus and the urethra. Some patients do not desire the vagina and are perfectly satisfied with the removal of the external genitalia only. This is a relatively simple one-step operation, but the production of a vagina may necessitate a two-step procedure. Techniques vary, but skilled operators can make a functioning vagina which may be difficult to distinguish from the "real McCoy" even with very close examination. It is lined with skin taken from the inside of the thighs, or with the skin from the amputated penis.

Many of the patients have claimed to have orgasm, and while this is impossible to substantiate beyond doubt, there is no reason to believe that it does not occur in some cases. All authorities agree that the female orgasm, although physiological at the end point, is primarily psychological in origin, and unlike the male orgasm, there is no easily observed evidence.

Estrogenic hormones may produce rather commendable breasts in males, but many of the transsexuals are not satisfied with what would otherwise be a normal bust measurement. Plastic transplants have become very popular with them, and some of them appear to rather overdo it in their zeal to demonstrate unmistakeably that they are female. This obsession with breast size is reminiscent of that seen in the homosexual culture's concern over penis size, and in some there is a fanatical desire for huge, protruding muscles.

Objective measurements of the success of such a drastic procedure as sexual transformation are difficult to obtain. This type of condition existing over a lifetime obviously should be expected to have adverse effects upon a personality already lacking total maturity, and it is not strange that many of them are relatively undependable and unstable people. Follow-ups, therefore, are not always easy to obtain, and the reliability of their reports may be questioned. However, most investigators report that between two-thirds and three-fourths of the results are very satisfactory. At least two-thirds of those with the artificial vagina report success in having sexual intercourse. Most operations are done upon men in their middle to late twenties; so it is expected that some relatively long-term follow-up will be forthcoming in the near future and that this follow-up will give us a more reliable basis for future evaluation.

The situation remains rather confusing from the legal standpoint. Sexual conversion obviously is elective plastic surgery with marked emotional overtones, and the tissues removed at surgery are not pathological and are not causing discomfort in the usual physical sense. There are conflicting views and many statutes that can produce nervewracking problems for the patient and his surgeon when reason and logic butt head-on with bureaucracy and red tape. It probably is best for the transsexual who seeks a conversion operation to investigate the legal aspects thoroughly prior to surgery, and if possible, to retain an attorney for this purpose. A full and happy life virtually necessitates that a court change of gender, including a birth certificate alteration be made. Without question, the operation should be discussed thoroughly with other significant family members, and they should be allowed to express their feelings after knowing all the facts.

The question of transsexualism and its corrective treatment touches upon many highly charged areas of living. Many of the questions that arise are unanswered or perhaps even unanswerable. It appears highly illogical to sentence an individual to a life of eternal misery if some hope of release is available. No one claims results of 100 percent satisfaction, but without intervention, it appears that the chance of any reasonably happy life is virtually nil. It is hoped that the future sees transsexualism become a purely medical question relatively free from the red tape of legal entanglements. We now accept surgical remodeling of noses, breasts, and aging faces, but the genitalia remain "sacred areas." Today's resistances are based far less upon logic than upon "gut" emotions which are aroused in most men by the thought of an elective castration, and most of our laws and regulations are made by men.

It is interesting that severe emotional reactions almost prevented plastic surgical repair of deformed noses prior to World War I. The same arguments were used then as are heard now about sexual transformation operations. It was said that tampering with nature was unethical and immoral, and surgeons who did so were medically ostracized in certain parts of Europe. The massive facial injuries of World War I necessitated plastic surgery, and after that, no more complaints were heard about it.

Prevention of transsexualism should be the eventual aim. Education of future parents may be the partial answer, but it is inconceivable that we will ever reach a state of being in which every parent is an emotionally stable, intelligent person. Until that is a reality, relief for the unhappy victims of today should be readily available without social and legal condemnation. This certainly will come with time. No one would have thought in 1940 that thousands of abortions would be performed openly and legally within thirty years. The changes in public attitude, then law, have happened with astonishing rapidity, and they are continuing to do so. The attitudes toward sexual change procedures will follow the same pattern. It will eventually come that a person's rights include the type of body the mind inhabits, whenever that is a possible choice. Prohibitions of this right, when they exist, should be based on scientific knowledge and not on an emotional bias. The sole criterion should be the functioning of the individual in the manner most consistent with personal fulfillment.

8

Fetishism

FETISHISM IS A sexual deviation in which an inanimate object or a body part is endowed with all the sexual significance usually attributed to the female genitalia. That object or body part is known as a fetish. A specific name, partialism, is used when the fetish is a particular part of the female body rather than the whole.

Fetishism may be one of the most common of the sexual deviations, but two factors make it difficult to obtain a clear idea of its frequency. First, since it does not involve another person directly in most instances, it is not in itself an illegal practice. Second, fetishism blends so imperceptibly into the normal that a line between the acceptable and the abnormal is difficult to draw in the more moderate cases. It appears obviously pathological when the object or body part involved is the primary source of sexual gratification, but to become deeply attached to some memento of a loved person or to become sexually stimulated by certain body parts or articles of clothing represents normal behavior.

Fetishism, per se, is a male deviation. Women may attach undue significance to a keepsake such as a lock of hair, a medallion, a ring, etc., but the major sexual element appears lacking. The use of male garments as masturbatory enhancements or as primary sexual stimulants is not reported.

The basic idea of a fetish without its obvious sexual

symbolism is found in all social groups, perhaps more so in those less civilized and sophisticated. Many American Indians wore their "medicine" into battle or on the hunt and attached great significance to it. Much of the success of the venture depended upon this "medicine." This object might be anything from a bird's wing to a collection of small stones, but some event had given it a special and highly individualistic meaning to that man. A sophisticated society may smile at such superstitution, but these fetishes do not differ from the saints' relics so highly revered in certain Catholic communities. In each instance, the symbolic object is endowed with power and meaning above and beyond its realistic function.

Forms of sexual fetishism also appear as old as man's written interest in sex. The erotic symbolism of the foot and its clothing, shoes and stockings, is mentioned by almost all of the earlier writers on sexual pathology. In some instances these fetishisms became integral parts of a given culture's pattern of living. For example, the Chinese attached tremendous importance to the female foot until very recent times. In referring to Chinese pornographic engravings of many years ago, Matignon wrote, "In all these lascivious scenes we see the male voluptuously fondling the woman's foot." The practice of binding the feet to prevent normal growth, cruel by modern Western standards, was designed to make them more sexually attractive to the male. Those who sneer at this barbaric practice should think of the tortures Western women will undergo at the beauty salon today.

Uncovering the feet of a person of the opposite sex has been considered a sexual act in many Eastern societies. This also was true of the ancient Jews and in the third chapter of Ruth, verse seven, it says, "And when Boaz had eaten and drunk, and his heart was merry, he went to lie down at the end of a heap of grain; and she came softly, and uncovered his feet, and laid her down." Ruth was telling

Boaz that she was his for the asking, and he, understanding her perfectly, married her shortly thereafter.

Shoes, female undergarments, and hair are the most common of the inanimate objects used as fetishes, but every known article is possible. Each object has in common that it is a symbol that produces erotic arousal and has a unique meaning in the unconscious of that individual. There is no universal agreement as to how a certain object becomes linked with sexual excitement, but the theory of Binet in 1888 remains plausible. He felt that it was purely accidental that some object happened to be available during a period or periods of intense sexual excitement in the young male, and that sexual excitement and that object thereby became permanently linked in the unconscious. This alone would not produce fetishism, but it might do so if the young male already had found the female genitalia so anxiety-provoking that he needed a neutral substitute for them. By the use of a symbolic object, the fetish, he becomes able to enjoy sexual stimulation to orgasm without confronting the "dangerous" vagina.

The basic personality of the fetishist sounds very much like that found in many of the other sexual deviants. He has a great doubt about his masculinity and an equal fear of rejection and humiliation by the female who is seen as a strong, devouring person. Some analytical authorities feel that this attitude develops because of strong unconscious fears of being castrated by the woman. The fetishist has experienced this anxiety initially in early childhood when discovering that the female did not possess a penis and making the erroneous conclusion that it had once existed but had been amputated as punishment for sins—sins which he feels that he also has committed. Contact with the female genitalia reawakens this anxiety and, therefore, must be avoided if possible.

Whether or not this type of anxiety is controlled by fetishism or exhibitionism, or even by a more obvious neurosis, may depend upon the chance conditioning as theorized by Binet. Also similar to many other disorders is the fetishist's underlying anger and rejection of the female. It is as if he is saying that a shoe, or a pair of panties, or whatever, is superior to the whole female. And yet, he has such great identification with the mother figure that he cannot bring himself to admit his negative feelings openly, but must express them in passive ways. That which he dislikes he also needs and does not consciously wish to offend.

Perhaps the best known fetishism is for female undergarments, especially panties. (The college panty raids of a few years ago had a faint fetishistic tinge.) Many young adolescents pilfer mothers' or sisters' panties and use them as tangible, erotic aids in masturbation. This stealing initially is necessary to avoid the embarrassment, shame, and ridicule that might come if his habit were known, but later it may become indelibly associated with the erotic component of the fetish. When this occurs, the fetishistic object has no stimulating power unless it is stolen. For example, a pair of panties purchased legitimately at a department store would be of no sexual value. Many men make collections of these stolen articles, and these collections have been referred to as "harems" in a facetious manner.

One young man of fifteen was brought to a consultation after being arrested for stealing panties in the neighborhood. He had been known to steal in this manner on several occasions, but no one had reported it to the police because of his reputation as a nice, quiet boy and because of the low value of the stolen objects. A new neighbor, unacquainted with the boy and his family, was not so lenient when he caught him taking panties from his daughter's bedroom. He physically restrained the boy while the police were called.

Over one hundred pairs of panties were found in the boy's room. They were locked in a trunk which his mother thought held only boyhood mementos and unused toys. Each of them showed evidence of soiling due to his habit of masturbating and ejaculating upon them as soon as possible after stealing them. His usual habit was to steal the panties, masturbate while holding them in his other hand, ejaculate on the panties, and then carefully stow them away, never to be used again. Almost half of the panties belonged to his mother. Could she have missed fifty pairs of panties, knowing that he had stolen panties from neighbors, and still remain without suspicion?

This young man was the only child of a very unhappy marriage. He had been thoroughly spoiled by his mother but virtually ignored by his father who referred to him as "her son" when the family was interviewed as a unit. His mother ruled the family with an iron hand and controlled it mostly by producing guilt and fear. Even though she had given her son everything he wanted materially, she had never given him individuality or self-esteem, the most important gifts of all. She was a coldly intellectual woman, a schoolteacher, who appeared unable to relate to him with genuine warmth and affection. She had never allowed him to engage in any of the usual childhood roughhouse play, all under the guise of preventing him from getting hurt. He had been allowed to engage in no extracurricular activities at school, and he had no friends of his own age. She had even walked to and from school with him almost every day until it became necessary for him to ride the bus when he entered junior high. Even after the arrest and the discovery of the "harem" of panties, his mother insisted that she could take care of the situation and that no assistance from the outside was needed. The court did not agree with her and remanded him for psychiatric consultation.

A complete psychiatric workup of this young man revealed a personality so deranged and immature and a family situation so abnormal that even with competent professional help his outlook for normal adult adaptation was very poor unless a major and improbable change occurred in the family.

This finding would indicate a need to treat the whole family conjointly, or to treat the parents and the boy separately, but simultaneously. Few families can afford this type of treatment, and in this particular case, no one was interested as soon as the kind old judge released the boy to his mother's care. He was never seen again.

Many fetishists show a level of maturity much higher than this young man, and they may appear to lead relatively normal lives to the casual observer. Mr. Grady was one such individual. He came to a psychiatric consultation upon the insistence of his wife who had come to realize that there was something abnormal about his sexual habits, although she had accepted them for two years.

Mr. Grady was a twenty-four-year-old mechanic, and his wife was a twenty-two year-old clerk in a department store. They had married two years previously after a courtship of one year. They had no children, and by good management they were buying a fairly nice home in a modern suburb. Both were high school graduates of average intelligence. In short, they appeared to be an attractive, average young couple who were assets to their community.

Their sexual activities had been confined to heavy petting prior to marriage by mutual, but unspoken agreement. Mr. Grady asked his new wife to allow him to undress her on the night of the wedding, and she complied willingly. He did not get this completed, however, and the first intercourse occurred with her still wearing her garter belt, stockings, and shoes. She rather appreciated his ardor, and it all seemed rather natural to her. She began to suspect something when the almost identical sequence of events occurred with each intercourse, and this occurred with normal frequency, for the next several days.

Mrs. Grady was a very naive and innocent girl, especially in sexual matters, but it gradually dawned upon her that her husband never made sexual advances toward her unless she were wearing high heeled shoes and silk stockings. He soon requested that she never wear anything except high heeled shoes and hose when he was home. She did not particularly like to wear the high heeled shoes around the house and the hose appeared to be an unnecessary expense, but she wore them to please him when he insisted that her legs looked so much better with them.

The pattern soon became obvious. Mr. Grady could not or would not have intercourse with his wife unless she were wearing silk stockings and high heeled shoes! No other form of stocking and shoe would suffice, and the totally nude body did not attract him. The mild annoyance this innocuous habit caused the young wife was more than compensated for by the kindness and attention she received from her husband. He was almost a sexual athlete as long as his modest requirements were met, and within a short length of time Mrs. Grady was having regular orgasms and their adjustment appeared ideal on the surface. This situation persisted for the first two years of marriage.

The local newspapers ran a feature series on sexual offenders. Rather lurid and sometimes inaccurate descriptions were given of most of the sexual deviations and the men who practiced them. One of the descriptions was of a man who combined fetishism and sado-masochism in a rather gruesome and improbable manner. Mrs. Grady had read these descriptions with interest, and unfortunately she saw a great deal of resemblance between her husband and the fetishistic male described in the newspaper article. The nagging doubts she had harbored about his habit now were fanned into overt concern by what she had read. She insisted that they speak to the family physician about it, and although he objected rather strenuously at first, Mr. Grady soon agreed. Thus it was that they came to be referred for psychiatric consultation after the family doctor had heard the story.

Mr. Grady was an engaging young man who, after his initial reluctance, appeared relieved to talk to someone about his condition. He was far more concerned about his inability to have intercourse with his wife under more average circumstances than he had admitted to her or even to himself. He had not actually become aware of the situation until after marriage. He, unlike Mrs. Grady, had not been a virgin at marriage, but all of his sexual experiences had been in the back seats of automobiles on country lanes. His sexual partners had remained as fully clothed as possible, and he had never seen a nude female prior to the wedding night.

The young man had known that shoes and silk stockings were fascinating to him for many years, but he had thought that it was perfectly normal to admire a well-turned calf clad in silk. However, some interesting childhood memories came out in subsequent interviews. One of these concerned the basement apartment in which he had lived as a very young boy. He could not remember exact ages, but he did recall that they had moved from this place before he began school at age five and one-half. All he could remember of this place was the small window exactly at the level of the sidewalk and only six inches away from it. He thought that he recalled spending many hours standing on a chest of drawers and watching the people pass by. The position of the window was such that he could not see far above the knees of the passersby, and it may have been significant that, as he told this story, he mentioned only the females and their legs. He recalled nothing sexualized about it at that time.

The family had moved from this basement apartment to a place which was surrounded by a high, dense hedge. He could not see over this hedge, but by squatting down, he could see the legs of people passing by through openings at the base. There was a nearby establishment that employed several young women. He made it a practice to station himself at the hedge when these young women were going to and from work, and as he watched their legs go by, he played with his erect penis with pleasure.

As he grew older, he recalled being fascinated by the mannequin displays of female shoes and stockings in department store windows. He remembered one particular store that specialized in female footwear as being a spot that would hold him spellbound for long periods of time. He began to masturbate with regularity at puberty, but always with either a picture of a female clad in silk sockings and high heeled shoes, or if a picture was unavailable, with the mental image of it.

Mr. Grady had been a relatively shy young man who, although he made friends rather easily, had dated very infrequently during high school. His few sexual encounters had been with girls known to be easy marks and with whom he did not have to make a close relationship. The woman who later became his wife was his first serious girl friend and her personality was much like his. He said that it never entered his mind to attempt to have intercourse with her prior to marriage; this was not a thing one did to nice girls.

Mr. Grady could not afford the intensive type of psychotherapy he needed from a private practitioner, so he was referred to the university clinic where it was available to him within his means. He had been in treatment for over a year at the last follow-up, and although he still preferred intercourse while his wife was wearing high heeled shoes and stockings, they were no longer an essential part of the sex act. His motivation to remain in therapy was unusual for a fetishist, and his prognosis was good.

Mrs. Grady was interviewed several times during the initial evaluation. She was concerned about her husband, but once she was assured that his condition was not dangerous to himself or others, she said that she could live with it if he could not be helped. She showed a delightful sense of balance and humor about the whole thing, and with a laugh, she said, "I really wouldn't mind so much if the high heels weren't so hard on the sheets!"

It is not possible even to mention, let alone describe, all the possible fetishes and the practices associated with them. Shoes, stockings, and female undergarments, especially panties, may be the most frequent, but not only is everything under the sun a possible fetish, even the absence of something can be one. For example, Havelock Ellis mentions the case of a man who was relatively impotent with normal women, but who experienced passion and affection for women who had lost a leg. He was able to make contact with many female amputees all over the country, and even though he did not meet most of them personally, he carried on an extensive correspondence with them and bought artificial limbs for many of them.

The use of a particular part of the female anatomy as a fetish, called partialism, was mentioned at the beginning of the chapter. One must distinguish this from the normal attraction certain parts of the female anatomy have for men. It is certainly no sign of fetishism to be erotically stimulated by a well-formed breast or buttock, and to be called partialism, this body part must become an end in itself. This means that a total female is unimportant, and that orgasm of a satisfactory nature can be obtained wtihout resort to intercourse so long as that body part can be touched, or in some cases, even viewed prior to masturbation. No section of the human anatomy is unknown to those who practice partialism. We have mentioned feet as partialistic objects, but one type of partialism, that involving the buttocks, is common enough to have a special name.

Frottage refers to partialism involving the buttocks. The meaning actually is a bit more narrowed in that it also signifies a condition in which the male feels compelled to rub against the buttocks of females, almost always strange ones, as if in an accidental manner. The man interested in frottage habituates crowded elevators, streetcars, subways, and other places where a crowd is certain to contain females and to be thick enough to excuse his apparently "accidental" contacts. He usually prefers to maneuver so that his erect penis rubs against the female's buttock, although some can obtain orgasm even if only their hip or thigh is in direct contact with the female anatomy. It is a harmless practice, at its worst annoying, and it is probable that it occurs far more frequently than the literature indicates. Urban crowding is such today that those interested in frottage do not lack opportunities!

There are some semiamusing aspects to fetishism. We mentioned earlier that stealing may be almost as important to the involved man as is the fetishistic object itself. At one time this dual need to steal and to obtain an article of female clothing was met almost entirely, and with considerable ease, from backyard clotheslines. Modern America has rapidly replaced the clothesline with the indoor dryer, thereby depriving many fetishists of their main source of sexual pleasure! It appears that progress always results in a hardship for somebody!

Fetishism, like so many of the deviations, represents a deepseated personality disorder, or perhaps more correctly, an obsessive-compulsive neurotic disorder. It is incompatible with complete heterosexual maturity, but it must be remembered that complete maturity is an ideal goal rarely reached. A minor fetishism may be quite consistent with a relatively normal and productive life. The degree of drive behind the fetishistic compulsion varies as greatly as does the meaning of the fetishistic object. The greatest danger of the condition is to the man himself. It frequently leads to shame and embarrassment, and sometimes even to legal difficulties.

One thirty-six-year-old man was embarrassed when he was brought to the emergency room in a semiconscious condition from a minor concussion resulting from his head striking the windshield of the car in which he was a passenger. He was a well-known citizen of the small community, and he had successfully hidden his fetish from his associates. The nurses who undressed him for the emergency room examination were surprised to find that he wore very fancy, lace-trimmed black panties! He recovered from his minor injuries very quickly, and he showed no interest in discussing his interesting habit!

This could have represented transvestism rather than fetishism, and only a history from the man would differentiate them. If he used the panties as a sexual end, that is, only as an aid to masturbation, then they probably were a fetish. On the other hand, if he wore them in order to admire himself or to be admired, they may have been a part of transvestism.

The preferred treatment for fetishism is group or individual psychotherapy, although some forms reportedly respond well to behavioral therapy in which the individual is "deconditioned" from the fetish. This may be of great assistance to the man, but it must be remembered that it will not banish the basic immaturity nor improve the personality deficits so frequently seen accompanying fetishism. Most fetishists are not made uncomfortable by their condition and they do not seek help voluntarily. When forced by wife or by legal authorities to seek treatment, they usually do so reluctantly for several months. Once they have been able to break through the resistance and to recognize that they are unhappy in their living patterns, and most of them are, they become well-motivated patients. This pattern is seen in sexual deviants over and over.

Fetishism usually becomes manifest in early adolescence. Punishment is irrational and ineffective. It should be recognized for what it is, a sign of severe sexual maladjustment. It is a mistake to think that it will be outgrown and to do nothing. Psychiatric consultation is mandatory, and the total family membership and interactions should be included in the work-up.

9

Sado-Masochism

SADO-MASOCHISM REFERS TO to the infliction of pain as a desirable prelude to, or as a necessary accompaniment of, sexual gratification. Sadism is the active, outwardly directed component in that the pain is inflicted upon the sexual object. Masochism is the passive, inwardly directed component in that the individual is the recipient of the pain. The predoleminent component, sadism or masochism, depends entirely upon the direction of the painful stimulus, away from or toward the individual in question. Because of this intimate association, we will discuss sadism and masochism as a unit rather than as separate conditions.

The two words, sadism and masochism, come from the names of two early novelists, the Marquis de Sade and Leopold von Sacher-Masoch. The Marquis de Sade was a French writer of stories mainly involving torture and cruelty. Von Sacher-Masoch was an Austrian novelist who frequently wrote of the subjugation of men by strong, malevolent women. History would have us believe that many of the words of these men were descriptions of personal experiences and desires, and there is much evidence to support this belief.

We use the words sadistic and masochistic in ordinary social relationships to refer to people who appear to enjoy inflicting pain and discomfort upon others, or to describe individuals who appear to be their "own worst enemies" or to "enjoy" a degree of suffering. Usage has made these concepts acceptable, but in neither case are we referring to the sexual deviation sado-masochism. This condition requires the inseparable marriage of violence, cruelty, pain, and lustful feeling.

Sado-masochism has existed as long as written history. There have been long periods of time in which some form of sado-masochism became so common as to be a way of life. The pleasure that many of the Romans obtained from witnessing the violence and cruelty of the arena appears unmistakably sexual. In 1487 two Dominican monks, Sprenger and Kramer, published a book called, *The Witches' Hammer* (Malleus Malficarum). This book delineates methods of detecting witches and describes in vivid detail what must be done to them. The intimate association of sadistic cruelty and sex forms the foundation of this horrible book that led to the deaths of hundreds of thousands of innocent people, mostly women, throughout Europe. The normal sexual fantasies of females became tickets to the executioner's block or to the fiery stake.

It is simpler to discuss sado-masochism if we break it into its component parts and treat each one separately. The reader must recall that they rarely stand alone in a given individual, although one of the impulses usually will be dominant at any given time.

Sadism

We have constantly referred to the normal facet of all the deviations we have discussed. There is no deviation, no matter how disgusting or repugnant it may seem, that does not have its root in some primitive aspect of human behavior that passes for normal or that was normal at some stage of development. So it is with sadism. Havelock Ellis stated, "The love bite may be said to give us the key to that perverse impulse which has been commonly called sadism." Would we wish to call every lover who has gained sexual pleasure from nibbling at his paramour's ear a sadist? But what if the nibble becomes a severe biting? It is worth discussing if only to illustrate how this normal phenomenon may pass insensibly into that which is morbid and deviant.

Many of the early writers appeared to think that sadism was active and therefore masculine and that masochism was passive and therefore feminine. This concept has long since been disproved as a generality, but it still tends to color our thinking because of the faint glimmer of truth in it. The thought that true masculinity is almost synonymous with strength, violence, and aggression is still very much alive in many segments of our society today. Equally alive, though perhaps slowly dying, is the idea that one truly arouses the love of the female only by the infliction of at least a little pain. The fact is that there is some truth in both of these concepts but that they are erroneous generalities. Many otherwise normal women will attest to occasional fantasies of how it would feel to be forcibly, if not brutally, treated.

The Marquis de Sade gave more than his name to the sexual deviation, sadism. He gave much of his life, and in the end gave his freedom when we consider that he spent almost twenty-seven years in prisons and asylums. Most modern researchers feel that the escapades of de Sade have been markedly exaggerated, and they rightfully feel that he wrote more from his fantasies than about his concrete actions. None, however, deny that his descriptions are so accurate and so sensitive that they could only have come from his own mind. There is much argument pro and con about pornography in our time, but de Sade's book *Justine*, written in 1781, is pornographic writing forever unexcelled. Most of the deviations are illustrated in a graphic manner possible only for an excellent writer who knew what he was talking about!

One paragraph from the writings of de Sade is worthy of repetition because it is so true of all the deviations. He said: "If there are beings in the world whose acts shock all accepted prejudices, we must not preach at them or punish them—because their bizarre tastes no more depend upon themselves than it depends on you whether or not you are witty, or stupid, well made or hump-backed—What would become of your laws,, your morality, your religion, your gallows, your paradise, your gods, your hell, if it were shown that such and such fluids, such fibers, or a certain acridity in the blood or in the animal spirits, alone sufficed to make a man the object of your punishments or your rewards?"

De Sade was saying, long before Freud, that we are not in command of our lives as much as we would like to think! He realized that the sexual deviations, and perhaps much of our behavior, were motivated from the unconscious, and largely uncontrollable, levels of the mind.

Montaigne once observed that cruelty was usually accompanied by feminine softness. This, like most generalities, is subject to question but certainly was true of the Marquis de Sade. As a youth he has been described as "of softly feminine grace" and as "an adorable youth whose delicately pale and dusky face [was] lighted up by two large black eyes." He became a handsome man, adept in the valued graces of his period and truly artistic in nature. Women adored him, and as he grew older, his reputation seemed to attract them rather than to repel them.

The development of sadism requires the linking of the aggressive and the sexual impulses quite early in life. Several factors may be operative, but one is that the young child perceives himself to be in danger of injury (castration) for real or imagined offenses. He protects himself by identifying with the presumed aggressor, usually a parent, and then in later life, when anxiety arises, he prevents it by symbolically or realistically harming others and thereby gaining the upper hand. He becomes the castrator instead of the castrated. Perhaps this is just another way of stating the military axiom that, "the best defense is a good offense."

The covert hostility toward and contempt for the female represented in sadistic men is perfectly obvious. This attitude may be reversed most of the time so that there is an oversolicitous attitude toward the female who is not seen as a sexual object. This was exemplified by the soft, gentle aspect of de Sade in everyday life. It may be that the sadist sees in the female love object an unacceptable part of himself and symbolically punishes or destroys it.

JM came for psychiatric consultation after his wife's father threatened to have him arrested if he did not do so. This father had discovered by accident that his daughter was being beaten with a leather belt rather unmercifully once or twice monthly. She initially concocted stories to account for the bruise marks over her body, but later she admitted that her husband was responsible for them.

JM at first refused to admit that his activities were anything other than perfectly normal, and he maintained rather irately that they were no concern of others. Even after he had faced the fact that this might not be so, he evidenced no discomfort or anxiety over them. His story, agreed upon by his wife, eventually came out: he was totally impotent unless he first inflicted pain upon the sexual object.

JM first noted the association of violence and sex in his middle teens. He had been a very attractive boy with a number of platonic girl friends. He was a shy boy, not very aggressive toward girls, and he dated only for parties or special functions. He remained virginal until after graduation from high school, but he had participated in petting, normal for his age at that time. He found that petting alone did not particularly arouse him, but that he invariably got an erection by pinching a girl until she screamed. He was even more excited if she gave evidence of pain and slapped him simultaneously. He masturbated frequently, and always with fantasies of inflicting pain upon an older female.

His first sexual experience occurred when he was a freshman in college. It virtually amounted to a rape in that he beat the girl about the head until she was almost unconscious. He had not intended a sexual advance at all, but during some playful scuffling he had accidentally hurt her. Her moaning and tears so excited him that he simply lost control and ended by having his first intercourse. She did not report this, in fact, they had frequent experiences thereafter! She considered it a sign of caveman virility.

JM married when he was in medical school. His scholastic career through college and into medical school was excellent, although slightly erratic, and he was felt to have a promising career ahead of him. He married a rather shy, withdrawn girl whom he knew to have a questionable reputation. By the time of marriage, in his middle twenties, he had become totally impotent unless he preceded the sexual act by some degree of violence. He no longer used his fists indiscriminately if he could avoid it but preferred to beat the back, buttocks, and thighs of the girl with an ordinary belt. He did not intend harm, but sometimes his exuberance led him to overenthusiasm and minor injury. He never failed to be genuinely contrite and apologetic when this occurred.

JM's parents were not available for an accurate history of his childhood. He described his mother as a seductive person who liked much body contact, but who was not actually interested in her son. (JM was an only child.) She was a long-suffering woman who tolerated continual abuse from a husband who was described as a man's man. It appeared to JM that his mother's only love was her husband, and that her love increased with his abuse of her. Despite his belief that his father was a physically cruel man, JM did not recall any undue physical punishment from him when he was a child.

His wife did not come to see her role in this sadomasochistic union. It seemed probable, had her father not accidentally discovered the situation, that she never would have reported it at all. Her explanation was that since he was impotent without this aggressive activity, she was willing to pay that small price for his sexual attentions. JM gave no rationalizations but rather simply stated that it was "his way." "His way," after he had aroused his erection through the beatings, was ordinary and, according to him and his wife, fairly active sexual intercourse, fully satisfying to both.

The acme of sadism is the lust murderer. This is closely related to necrophilia, a condition to be discussed in another chapter, but it must be mentioned here also. It involves killing and sometimes the mutilation of the corpse for the achievement of sexual gratification. Some have sexual intercourse with the victim after the killing, and some may not. Some, as was said of the Boston Strangler, kill then masturbate upon the victim. Others, as was attributed to Jack the Ripper, get their sexual satisfaction from the murder alone. They leave little doubt about their inner feelings and attitudes towards females!

JB was a twenty-four-year-old young man so deeply and pathologically attached to his mother that he had never had one single date in his life without her presence. He was an adopted child and there were no other children in the family. He knew nothing of his actual parentage, but his fantasy was that his mother was a very wealthy and refined woman who had given him away because he was too much trouble. He denied any fantasies about his real father. His adopted father was a traveling man who apparently avoided home whenever possible, and who had demonstrated absolutely no affection for the child. His mother appeared to have created a life in which there was no room for anyone except JB and herself. Her over-protectiveness was unbelievable even to psychiatrists who are accustomed to seeing it in the extreme.

JB at twenty-four lived alone with his mother in a small northeastern town. He worked in a drycleaning plant near home and spent his leisure time watching television, walking, or going to movies with his mother. Having never been alone with any females except his mother, he was still a virgin.

JB masturbated an average of three times weekly. His favorite fantasy while masturbating was to imagine sliding a large kitchen knife into the vagina of a woman while she was standing, then to see if he could cut her into two equal halves by one tremendous upward thrust! Another fantasy which aroused him sexually involved women being burned at the stake á la Joan of Arc.

One evening JB attended a circus with his mother. Before leaving the house he secreted a large kitchen knife in his inside coat pocket. He felt this knife while at the circus, picked out an attractive young girl performer, and imagined how it would be to try his fantasy on her. He got a very pleasant and gratifying erection from this, and thereafter, he made it a rather frequent occurrence to carry the knife and to fantasize his gory act on the girls he saw.

These feelings so frightened him that he confided in his mother a few months later. She refused to take him seriously and laughed at the idea that he might need help or that he could ever harm anyone. His belief in her infallibility allayed his fears, but for a time he gave up carrying the knife at her request.

JB's mother was hospitalized and operated upon for a possible cancer of the uterus. JB was alone for the first time in his life, since his father came home only for the day of the surgery. On the night of the third postoperative day, he took the knife and drove aimlessly around town in his mother's car. He happened to be passing an apartment by sheer chance when he saw a young girl get out of a car and enter the front door. He recognized her as a customer of the drycleaning establishment in which he worked, and he knew that she was single and that she lived alone. There was no plan and no premeditation, but he felt compelled to follow her. JB said that he knocked upon the door and told her that he wanted to talk to her. She recognized him and let him in without question. Remember, he was a very quiet and likeable chap who would arouse no suspicion in those who knew him. Either he could not or he would not recall exactly the details of the act, but in any event, JB did not carry through the fantasy he had had for so long. He attempted to do so, but in the ensuing struggle, he killed her with a stab wound in the abdomen. Then he stabbed her over and over again, more than fifty-six times according to the autopsy report. Making little or no attempt to avoid detection or to cover his bloody trail, JB went home, washed, put his gory clothing in the washing machine, and had a good night's sleep. He could not even recall whether or not he masturbated with his usual fantasy!

JB regretted his act. His regret was almost academic, however, and there appeared to be no true remorse, guilt, or anxiety. His conscious regret was more over the effect his arrest would have on his mother than over what he had done to the girl. The arrest had come quickly, and JB made a full confession. He requested psychiatric help, and he was seen in consultation at the request of the court. Legally, JB was perfectly sane, and he was sentenced to life in prison. He was genuinely hurt that the court did not see fit to release him to psychiatric care, and he felt that society had treated him unjustly.

Masochism

It has been theorized that a degree of masochism is a normal feminine trait. It is pointed out that the woman is by sexual nature a "passive recipient." The loss of virginity supposedly is attended by pain, and the discomfort and agonies of childbirth are a part of Biblical lore. These concepts no longer receive much credit, and masochism is not considered to be either normal or feminine. The childhood origins of the condition apparently stem from the Oedipal conflict during which much unconscious guilt is developed. Pain and suffering become an atonement in which the guilt is magically alleviated. (Note the use some religions make of this concept.) It also may be that the masochist needs to suffer repeated damages to his body (symbolic castration) in order to keep reassuring himself that he is not in fact damaged or castrated. In any event, discomfort and pain become inseparably associated with sex.

Leopold von Sacher-Masoch was a very delicate infant who was not expected to live. He probably would not have survived had his mother not given him to a Russian peasant woman who became not only his wet nurse but who remained forever his mother figure. It was noted that he was greatly attracted to pictures of cruelty even when a child. He later stated that one of his regular dreams after puberty was of being tied and tortured by a cruel and powerful female.

A biographer of von Sacher-Masoch tells of a traumatic boyhood experience that supposedly occurred in his tenth year. He developed a boyhood crush on one of his father's relatives, a beautiful but totally undisciplined woman. He was allowed to assist her in her dressing room, and while doing so, he became fascinated by some of her clothes, especially her furs. It is with her that he may have had his first masochistic experience. Once, while he was helping her put on her shoes, he impulsively kissed her foot. She kicked him forcefully on the body and produced a pain which filled him with pleasure. Not long after this he accidentally saw her in an episode in which she thoroughly and unmercifully beat her own husband with a large leather whip. The sexual excitement of this scene became indelibly engraved upon his memory, and fur garments and whips, both connected with this fantasied love of his youth, remained forever his favorite emotional symbols. They assumed an importance to him that bordered upon the fetishistic.

Von Sacher-Masoch married and became a father. His wife was a relatively normal woman who could not cooperate fully in his bizarre sexual desires. He finally succeeded in forcing her into intercourse with another man, but soon after this she left him in disgust. He ended his life living with another woman in a small town where he became a fairly honored philosopher. This man was described as, "Apart from his sexual eccentricities, he was an amiable, simple, and sympathetic man with a touchingly tender love for his children." His wife reported that another woman said of him, "He was as simple as a child and as naughty as a monkey."

Von Sacher-Masoch needed to be subjugated by powerful women, and yet, his very activities were a way of ruling the female. By reducing the woman to the whip-wielder, he was exerting control over her. Did he see all women as symbols of the mother who gave him away, and was he trying to get revenge upon them? Or did he see himself so evil and so degenerated that he needed the woman (mothers) to punish him? It is probable that both these components interacted in von Sacher-Masoch.

Mr. F was a junior executive with an insurance company. He was married to an extremely attractive woman, had an expensive home, two cars, and two children. He came to consultation at his wife's insistence because she felt that his practice might have some influence on the children who were now four and six years of age.

They had married when both were in their early twenties after a two-year courtship. She specifically had been attracted to him because he was so unlike the other boys she had known in college. He made no sexual demands upon her, and he was almost storybook in his kindness and gentleness toward her. She, who had known a life with a very boisterous and aggressive father who delighted in beating up the family while drinking, felt that she had found the perfect mate in this chivalrous young man.

She was disappointed on the wedding night and thought that perhaps he carried his passivity too far. He did not touch her. He later said that he did not wish to force himself upon her, so there was no sexual intercourse until the second week of the marriage. Thereafter it occurred at two to three week intervals for the next three or so years.

She had thought their sex life to be a bit low-keyed for her, but she did not become concerned about it until the third or fourth year of the marriage. He began to make more and more insinuations until he openly suggested that it would be all right with him if she had an outside affair. His liberal and generous attitude did not please her, but she was even more surprised by the request he made shortly thereafter. He asked her to tie him tightly, totally nude, to a kitchen chair. She objected to this, but after some discussion and persuasion on his part, she did it. He insisted that the rope be so tight as to be painful, but after about twenty minutes he requested to be untied. During this time he developed a healthy erection! He then had intercourse with her, rather more vigorously than usual, for the first time in several weeks. Nothing was said of this for about three months, and then the whole scheme was repeated. He was most insistent that the rope be tight enough to leave marks upon him for some time. He asked her to hit him in the face, but this she refused to do.

Their relationship stayed at this level until they came for the consultation a few years later. The only change was that he had become more and more insistent that she take up with a lover, and he seemed pleased that she did have one brief affair, which she confessed to him in detail. He confessed that he had no ambition to do this himself, and that he would remain totally faithful to her. She had gradually lost most of her feeling for him, and although he wished to continue the relationship, she soon insisted upon a divorce.

Some people apparently discover the masochistic element in themselves almost by accident. This was the case of Z, a homosexual college student who came for consultation at the request of her roommate and lover. Z, like many homosexual people, claimed that she had always been that way. She had suffered through many agonizing crushes upon female teachers and girl friends during high school, but she had not had an overt sexual relationship until a freshman in college. She and her roommate had engaged in mutual masturbation and cunnilingus for the first year of their relationship, but Z never found the sexual aspects of their love very exciting. She enjoyed doing things for her lover and appeared almost to want to enslave herself to her, but that was the extent of her needs.

The discovery of her masochistic impulses came one evening when she and her lover were horseplaying in the shower room of the dormitory. They were flicking at each other with moist towels when the roommate got in a couple of very painful licks on her buttocks. She immediately became aware of an intense pleasureful feeling mingled with the pain, and then a greater than usual sexual desire flooded over her. She immediately dragged the roommate to bed and, in Z's words, "for the first time I really knew what love was all about!"

Z repeatedly initiated the towel flicking episodes in the shower room until the roommate became exasperated with it, and it had become obvious that Z was using this as a source of sexual stimulation. When the roommate confronted Z with this, Z had the first conscious realization of what was happening. She then asked her roommate to beat her with a wet towel and when this was done, she achieved even greater sexual stimulation than she had thought was possible.

Had the roommate been happy about continuing this relationship, nothing would have been heard of it. Fortunately or unfortunately as the case may be, she was taking a course in abnormal psychology and a discussion of sexual deviations enlightened her as to what was happening to Z. It was then that she insisted that Z seek psychiatric consultation, and since Z refused to do this alone, they came together.

Z came from a very fundamentalistic rural home in which her father ruled the household with an "iron fist in a velvet glove." She was the apple of her father's eye, and she adored this man whom she saw as a paragon of strength and virtue. One of her rationalizations for never dating males was that there were none who could come up to the standards she set for a man—to be like her father. Her father treated her with a strictness unusual for today, but she felt that this only demonstrated his love for her.

Her mother was a mousey, nondescript woman who waited upon the daughter and husband hand and foot. Z was consciously aware of her mother's dislike, perhaps even hatred for her, and she felt that it was because her mother knew that the father loved his daughter more than his wife. Z had literally won the Oedipal battle with her mother, but she had done so at a high price. By no means was this the whole answer, but part of Z's need to be punished was due to the guilt she felt over having defeated her mother. Another faction of Z's masochism came from her unconscious desires to gain her mother's love, a thing she actually never had. By subjugating herself to another female who represented the mother figure, symbolically she hoped to achieve both the love and the punishment.

Sado-masochism must not be confused with simple cruelty. Obviously there is a relationship between the two, but they are far from synonymous. Cruelty can exist without an overt sexual component and without being classed as a deviation of a sexual impulse. A cruel father or mother can influence a child to act the same in adulthood, but it is feasible for this facet of behavior to remain separated from sex.

The sado-masochist may be of no danger to society, or he may be a terrifying menace when the sadistic impulse gains supremacy. The fact that a sadist is emotionally ill is of little comfort to his victim or the relatives. Prediction of this destructive behavior is precarious but frequently possible at a fairly early age. As we saw in the stories of de Sade and von Sacher-Masoch, there was a certain personality constellation. We do not know all the past history, but we might have seen a triad of firesetting, bedwetting, and cruelty to animals or other children. These three behavioral aspects are seen as danger signs in a child and they should be taken as signals that something is going awry. Modern techniques of family and child therapy probably could prevent the de Sades of the world, but treatment after the condition has fully developed is not so promising. Detention may be essential to protect society, but the milder cases may harm no one except themselves.

Outpatient treatment of the severe cases in adulthood is a hazardous undertaking. However, as in the case of JB, there would have been no way to predict the unfortunate outcome from his ordinary behavior. Most of these cases come to attention only after some act has gotten them into trouble with the law or their families.

Men like JM, the wife beater, are not apt to extend their activities beyond their mates, and they ordinarily do not commit lust murders or crimes against society. Their afflictions may cripple their own lives and cause their families discomfort, but they are not involved with the law very often. Their everyday lives may proceed with little indication of their sexual peculiarity. We have no way of knowing how many people are afflicted with this personality disorder, but we are certain that most of them do not come to medical attention.

These unfortunates frequently are medico-legal problems of some magnitude. Society deserves protection from them, yet we do not like to punish those not responsible for their acts. Those who are of most danger, the lust murderers, do not do well with presently known methods of treatment and incarceration is necessary. Those less severe may be treated as outpatients by either group or individual psychotherapy, but by far the best results are obtained by the treatment of children and their families before the condition becomes fixed.

10

Rape

RAPE IS AN act of sexual intercourse performed with a female, not the wife of the perpetrator, without her consent. Rape, by this definition, is not always a sexual deviation. We shall see that several forms of rape, while representing some degree of personality pathology, are not true deviations.

There are some cultures in which the forceful subjugation of the female for sexual purposes is not looked upon with the same horror found in Western civilizations, and this leads some authorities to call rape a cultural deviation. For it to be classed as a true sexual deviation there must be the element of impulsive and compulsive behavior, and the forceful aspect of it must be an essential part of the sexual gratification. A man who in anger forced intercourse upon a female he felt had encouraged him would have committed legal rape and displayed poor judgment, but he would not necessarily be a sexual deviate.

The definition above is inaccurate in that it does not include homosexual rape. This probably is an infrequent occurrence in ordinary life, but it is by no means rare in our prisons, as many young, handsome men, newly committed, can testify. Even though homosexual rape is a well recognized part of prison life, it is virtually impossible to prevent as long as society wishes to punish rather than to rehabilitate persons convicted of crimes.

We will not concern ourselves with statutory rape—sexual intercourse with a girl younger than the age of consent—nor with cases in which there is an element of force or aggression associated with intercourse with a willing partner. Neither will we be concerned with the sadistic aspect of some rapes because, as previously discussed, that would imply that the infliction of pain was a necessary part of the gratification. Rape, as a separate sexual deviation, is not designed to inflict pain, and if it does so, it is purely incidental. Neither does the rapist wish only to achieve sexual intercourse. He well may be married and leave an attractive wife's bed in order to commit the act. It is the aspect of force that is significant to the true deviant rapist.

The true incidence of rape is unkown. It is estimated that less than half the cases are reported to the authorities. Raped women frequently do not wish to face the publicity and embarrassment, and at other times they do not want to face the fact they have encouraged or invited the crime. Our society, liberal as it may be, considers the raped woman to be defiled and damaged far beyond the significance of the act. This appears true even when no particle of blame can be attached to her.

Murder may be associated with rape under certain circumstances, but rarely enters into the discussion of rape as a deviation. Lust murder was mentioned as a part of sadomasochism. In these cases the sexual deviate was driven to inflict pain rather than to force intercourse on his victims. When a rapist murders, it is because he fears the social consequences of his act and hopes to avoid detection and identification by getting rid of the person who can identify him. This usually represents a panic reaction unassociated with the original impulse or with the process of gratification.

Rape is considered one of the most heinous of crimes in Western civilization, and few acts will arouse so much righteous indignation in a community. Even the suspicion of rape has caused many brutal and senseless lynchings in the past. Even though there is considerable question about the validity of many rape charges, the popular reaction to them almost invariably is a marked overreaction. Such overreaction always makes us suspicious that it represents a defense against similar impulses in the overreactor! Most men might not wish to admit this, but fantasies of raping are quite common, especially in adolescence and young adulthood, and this is the predominant age bracket of rapists. We even like to rationalize that most women find the forceful aggressive man more attractive than the considerate and gentle one.

Many motivating factors must come together to produce the true rapist. He must feel inferior in his masculine role and must conceive of himself as unable to conquer the female without force. He becomes compelled to assure himself of his male dominance by a show of aggression. As a "fringe benefit," his act places the female victim in a position of degradation and shame. Thus, he is able to express his hostile feelings toward women, whom he tends to see as evil and untrustworthy sexual objects. To oversimplify, the rapist conceives of sexual intercourse as something that no individual engages in voluntarily—especially with him!

It is completely erroneous to consider the rapist an oversexed person. Nothing could be further from the truth. His sexual life usually has been heavily weighted toward fantasy, and he tends, like other deviates, to be an underachiever in all aspects of life. Most rapists come from the lower socioeconomic strata of society.

The rapist's victim frequently represents a substitute for his mother, toward whom he had unfulfilled incestuous desires in early youth. A mother certainly would not allow her son to have sexual intercourse with her; so the attack to overcome her resistance is necessary. This carries with it the implied fantasy that she really wants the act to occur but that she is unable to subdue her own personal inhibitions and to sidetrack the social condemnations against it. Many rapists actually feel that they have been of benefit to the victim, and they may have some difficulty in understanding why she does not show the appropriate gratitude. Some have been so confident that their "loving" was a treat for the woman that they have returned to the scene of the crime expecting forgiveness and acceptance.

The acts of rape are quite as variable as are the men who do them. Intercourse is usual, but other degrading or humiliating acts may be included. Forced fellatio occurs in about one-fourth of rapes, and repeated sexual entry occurs in almost one-half the cases. Humiliating acts are far more common when the rape is performed by two or more men working in concert (the gang or group rape).

The following case represents a most unusual type of rape, one which never appeared on the court records. It graphically illustrates the significance of force in the act of rape. This young couple sought consultation upon the insistence of the wife, and at last report, the young man was still in treatment with the psychiatrist to whom he was referred.

This couple, both college students, were married when he was twenty-one and she was twenty. Both were highly religious members of a very fundamental religious sect. Both were ultrapuritanical in their moral standards, and as a result, they had not gone beyond hand holding and kissing before marriage. He made no sexual advances on their wedding night and she was very grateful because she saw this as a sign that he loved her so much that he was restraining himself. They spent the wedding night comfortably and pleasantly cuddled in each other's arms. This appeared so natural to her that many days had passed before she began to realize that a gradual increase in his sexual advances was not occurring as she had expected it would.

The young bride questioned a married friend just

enough to decide that something was amiss in her marriage. She spoke to her bridegroom about his lack of sexual interest in her, but he assured her that he was restraining himself because of his great regard for her and that too much haste in this part of marriage would unwisely jeopardize their future. The sexual aspect of their union, he assured her, would come naturally when they had adjusted completely to living together. She accepted this explanation rather reluctantly and continued to be a patient, but virginal, wife.

The young couple went on a picnic in the mountains in September following their June wedding. They leisurely enjoyed lunch at a secluded spot; then he dozed off in the comfortable sunshine of early fall. She wandered idly about the rugged area leaving him to his siesta. Without warning she suddenly felt herself hurled to the ground, and before she discovered her assailant was her husband, she was struggling, scratching, and screaming in alarm. There, in a rocky ravine on the side of a mountain, she lost her virginity and also some of her skin!

The young husband was genuinely contrite over the fact that his wife had suffered some minor bruises and scratches. He apologized profusely for this, but he rationalized his part of the episode as "playful," and his apologies were not for the act itself but for the fact that he had been too rough on her. She was confused and frightened by the incident, but there was something gratifying about it and she was able to join him in his rationalizations. Their relationship was strained and a little awkward for a day or two, but it quickly regained its old close, but platonic, status quo.

The wife had secret expectations and hopes that this incident would mark the beginning of a normal marital relationship. These hopes gradually dwindled over the next three weeks; so she once again raised the subject with her husband. Although he had discussed it quite calmly previously, this time he appeared short-tempered and irritable and would not talk about it. She did not push him and was somewhat alarmed by this change in his usually imperturbable self.

One can speculate about the motivations behind it, but on the next weekend the young couple again picnicked near the same area in the mountains. Perhaps it was a conscious desire on her part to see what would happen if he were again placed in the same situation, or perhaps it was a way of testing him. It may even have been totally unconscious, but in any event, the act was repeated in almost exactly the same manner—except this time she did not scream.

The young wife could not quell her anxieties any longer, and although she was upset and embarrassed by it, she confided once more in her married friend. Her friend expressed horror and alarm, assured her that her husband was mentally ill, and encouraged her to leave him immediately. This she could not do and could not seriously consider, but she did use the threat of separation as a method of getting him to agree to psychiatric consultation.

Although we do not know enough about this young man to make a definitive statement about his motivation, he seemed to be deeply embued with the idea that women were puritanical and angelic that he could not associate sexuality with them. He viewed sexual intercourse as the epitome of evil and his wife as the epitome of good. He could not believe that she would voluntarily submit to something so shameful and degrading as sexual intercourse, and yet he could not constrain his own impulses. This does not fully explain his psychopathology, nor does it explain why, in all of the other opportunities he had with her, he chose the secluded spot in the mountains. The uncivilized wildness of the location may have triggered his own primitive aggressive impulses, but this is only speculation.

Aggression and hostility were repressed in this young man as thoroughly as was sexuality. He was quiet and passive to a fault; so much so that he considered even the feeling of anger a major sin. He denied ever having felt anger toward any human being. Even if he felt himself to be willfully wronged by another person, he merely considered that as one of God's ways of testing him. And yet his attack upon his wife showed unquestionable aggressive urges toward the females!

The relationship of rape to unresolved feelings toward the mother was mentioned. Some cases demonstrate this with clarity. The story of one young man who was interviewed several times while serving a long prison sentence for raping a woman over twice his age is illustrative. He first came to psychiatric attention because of the repeated physical mistreatment he received from the other prisoners. Inmates who have raped old ladies do not win popularity polls in penitentiaries!

RB had been working as a bag boy at a supermarket for two years when he first encountered his future victim. She was a lady who appeared to be about fifty years of age and who always treated him with motherly kindness when he helped her with her groceries. They became quite friendly over a period of months, and RB learned that she was a widow whose only son had been killed early in the Vietnamese war.

One evening she was the last customer to leave the supermarket. RB insisted upon carrying her groceries home for her since it was on his regular route to his house. She invited him in for a cup of coffee, and he readily accepted. It was not until this moment in the relationship that RB became consciously aware of the fact that he was sexually attracted to her. Prior to that moment he had considered her only as a kind mother figure he enjoyed helping. She was unaware of his change in attitude toward her. When he made some obscene remarks to her, she ordered him to leave in surprised anger. He then struck her viciously in the abdomen with his fist. The breath was knocked out of her completely, and before she recovered sufficiently to scream,

RB had ripped off her underclothing and was proceeding to rape her. He threatened to kill her if she screamed, but after he had finished raping her, he remained with her almost an hour trying to calm her. He appeared to consider the rape a minor, mischievous act and to be surprised that she was so upset. He pleaded with her not to tell anyone, and he promised repeatedly never to do it again. Since she was petrified with fear, she told him she agreed to forget it. But as soon as RB left the house, she called the police. RB was arrested and had confessed within an hour.

The routine psychological testing and interviewing that was given RB in the prison to which he was sentenced for twenty years showed a borderline I. Q. in a young man obsessed with ambivalent feelings towards his mother. He openly manifested great love and concern for her, but his strong negative feelings were very close to the surface. It also showed an extremely poor masculine identification and a generally immature personality structure with a borderline ability to assess reality. The tests, added to the psychiatric interviews, strongly suggested a borderline or latent schizophrenic male of low intelligence.

RB had been raised partly by his mother and partly by a sister five years his senior. There was some uncertainty about his legitimacy, although he had been told that his father had died before his birth. He recalled a constant string of boyfriends his mother had entertained, frequently in his presence. Most of his life he had slept with his mother, when the bed was not occupied by one of her male friends. When he was small, he slept on a cot in the corner of his mother's room when her bed was not available. When he grew older, he was relegated to sleeping on the divan in the living room just outside his mother's bedroom door. He could not recall the number of times he had witnessed his mother having sexual intercourse, but he did remember once being severely beaten by one of his mother's customers when it was discovered that he had invited some young acquaintances in to watch the show through the keyhole! His mother was not overly concerned about this, however, and it was soon forgotten. In fact, once she had gotten over her initial anger, he recalled that she had considered it a laughing matter.

By the time RB was sentenced to prison in his twenty-second year, his mother had degenerated into severe alcoholism, too old and too unattractive to continue the life she had known in his childhood.

RB had been a very slow learner in school, and this, combined with his severe degree of shyness and his home situation, had made it very difficult for him to make and to hold friends. His sister had long since moved out of the home, leaving him to care for his alcoholic mother. His major concern about being in prison was what would become of his mother now that he was no longer there to care for her. He had ben imprisoned for almost six months by the time of the psychiatric interviews, but she had visited him only one time although she lived only sixty miles away. Once every three to four weeks she sent him a bedraggled postcard. Each card repeated with regular monotony how tough life was on her since RB had gotten himself into trouble. The refrains were "How could you do this to me?" and "What will become of me now?"

RB, like many of the men who choose rape objects much older than themselves, had expressed his vengeful feelings toward the mother who had betrayed him with other men. He had been able to get revenge in a dual fashion—both symbolically and realistically. His victim symbolized the mother towards whom he could not consciously express his hate, aggression, and contempt. Realistically, he punished his mother because his imprisonment destroyed his mother's sole source of support and left her completely alone. Simultaneously, the rape had expressed the sexual desires he had felt as a young boy watching his mother have intercourse.

RB was a model prisoner; therefore, he probably will be paroled when he is about thirty-two years of age. He will not have received the psychiatric help he needs; it simply is not available. Even if good treatment were available, it would be impossible to say whether or not RB would repeat his crime because true rape does tend to be repeated. His sexual fantasies in prison were exactly the same as those he had had ever since puberty: he masturbated while mentally picturing older women who were resisting, yet secretly enjoying it. Perhaps these fantasies in RB will change spontaneously with the years. Let us hope so.

The young bridegroom and RB illustrate another facet of rape. In almost one-half the cases of rape, the victim is acquainted with the offender, and the National Commission on Crime and Violence reports that 10 percent of rapes occur between family members. By no means is rape confined to the stranger prowling about for an unknown victim.

One must discuss the role of the female in rape in order to get a complete picture of it. Those familiar with the psychological and legal aspects of rape are only too familiar with the frequency with which the female, either wittingly or unwittingly, entices and encourages the rapist. These women frequently are unconsciously encouraging rape to prevent themselves from having feelings of guilt. They are unable to have normal sexual intercourse without guilt feelings because they have been taught that sex is sinful. However, they feel that if they are taken against their will by force and violence, then obviously they cannot be blamed. They, like the rapist, see the sexual act as something not to be done voluntarily by females.

Other women lay themselves open to rape almost as if they feel that they deserve that type of punishment. It is as if they seek it as atonement for sins committed in the past in fact or fantasy—more often the latter. For example, one college girl made a practice of wandering about dark alleys at all hours of the morning in a section of town known to be unsafe at any time. Her reasoning was that she could not sleep and that she enjoyed the solitude. This young girl was a guilt-ridden, inhibited, and sensitive person apparently unaware of the meaning of her behavior. She saw herself as a very unattractive girl, but she had fantasies of being abducted by a strong, forceful man who would turn her into a lovely, sexualized woman.

Another such woman was picked up by a rather well-dressed, muscular male at a bar one afternoon. She allowed him to buy her a couple of drinks and then to walk her to her home a few blocks away. She invited him into her apartment, where she lived alone, for another drink. He had finished about one-half his drink when he became such an insistent wooer that she indignantly ordered him out of the apartment. He refused to go and began to force the issue with more vigor. At this point she threatened to scream and bring the police. With an oath of digust he walked out the door and started down the steps. She came to the door and called after him, "You might as well come back and finish your drink before you leave." With that he returned to the apartment and raped her despite her unfulfilled threats to scream for help. Somehow he sensed that her threats were idle.

The woman filed charges against him, and he was arrested the next day. This story was obtained when he was seen in the psychiatric examination ordered by the court. Her testimony was almost identical with his, although at first she denied having asked him to return to finish his drink. She later appeared to lose interest in prosecuting him and then recalled that his version was substantially correct. One reason why she lost interest in pushing the case may have been a fact turned up by his lawyer—this was the second time that she had been "raped" within two years, and there was great similarity between the two incidents.

This vignette was used to illustrate the role the female plays in some cases of rape, but this man's story also is worth a brief look. He was thirty-eight years of age and a truly handsome, muscular individual. He had been a professional baseball player of moderate success between the ages of twenty-three and thirty-four. After retiring from the sports' world, his life gradually disintegrated. He had gone unsuccessfully from one job to another. His wife finally had separated from him taking their two children. At the age of thirty-eight he felt like an old and lonely man with neither present nor future. Perhaps the crucial point in his story was that his sexual potency had declined gradually since his retirement from baseball until he had become virtually impotent.

There was no question about his act from the legal viewpoint. It was rape. But there is rape, and there is rape! It is difficult, however, to get the unconscious of the victim to testify before a jury, and the law does not allow the moral standards of the woman to influence its definition of rape. Even the worst prostitute has the right to choose her customers! The law usually considers the circumstances surrounding the act, however. In the case discussed above, the man was found guilty but was given a short suspended sentence with the requirement that he enter psychiatric treatment.

The rapist is a sick man; that is obvious. Most of the time he is not psychotic, but his emotional illness may be complicated by other circumstances, such as the borderline intelligence of RB. Some few may have demonstrable brain damage or other conditions that reduce impulse control. This places society in a double bind. It does not wish to incarcerate and punish a man for that which is obviously beyond his control, and yet it cannot allow its citizens to be subjected to his impulsive actions. The rapist needs treatment, but he may be a poor candidate for outpatient therapy where so little control can be exerted over his activities. He is even more dangerous if undue violence has been associated with his act.

Alcohol frequently is implicated in rape, but it is not a causative factor. The rapist may prime himself with a few drinks in order to alleviate his anxiety and to lower his inhibitions, but drinking itself does not make a man a rapist. Neither does the use of drugs. They are more apt to reduce sexual impulses and drives; in fact, the unconscious desire to be asexual may be one motivation for drug use. We use the word *fiend* to describe those who misuse drugs and sex (dope fiend, sex fiend), but there is little or no direct connection between drugs and sex and none between drugs and rape.

The court has a difficult decision to make when it must decide the fate of these poor men. Each case must be considered individually, and even then society must be prepared to take some gamble. Incarceration for some time may be essential, but it appears equally essential that these men be treated while in detention so that repetitions can be avoided after release, if possible.

It is not germaine to rape as a deviation, but the homosexual rapes of prison society might be reduced noticeably if conjugal visits were allowed. This has been the experience when this enlightened practice has been tried, e.g., in Mississippi and some states in Mexico. The prevention of heterosexual rape is more complex. One preventive measure frequently preached is for women to avoid strangers, dark places, etc. This is good advice, but remember that the rapist and his victim are frequently acquainted and that the victim's home is the single most frequent site of rape. Accepting rides or drinks from strange men is an open invitation to rape. In general, the prevention of rape must be with the rapist, not simply with the victim. Sexual education and reform alone will not do it, nor will anything until we have the utopia of well-adjusted parents raising children they love.

11

Incest

INCEST REFERS TO sexual relations with a close relative. It is not, strictly speaking, a sexual deviation, but as will be seen, it bears a close relationship to pedophilia, and it is legally a sexual offense. Almost every society has a taboo against some form of incest even though the proscriptions may vary in type and degree from place to place. The most universal taboo is that which forbids sexual relations between parent and child, but the absolute taboo concerns relations between mother and son.

The fact that many societies take very elaborate precautions against incest can only indicate that the inclination toward it is rather strong and that the social consequences have been considered disastrous. For example, in many primitive groups, brothers and sisters are forbidden to speak directly to each other or even to come into any form of bodily contact after the age of puberty.

The early Egyptian civilization gives us one of the few instances of legally and morally sanctioned incestuous relationships between parent and child. The power of the throne literally descended in the female line from mother to son; therefore, a Pharaoh without a male child might try to produce one by his oldest daughter in order to insure his lineage. Actual marriages between father and daughter reputedly occurred, but these may have been more legal maneuvers than social ceremonies. It appears that Akhenaten, the eighteenth dynasty Pharaoh who so resembled Jesus Christ in his philosophy, and who was the first to espouse monotheism, impregnated one of his daughters, but that the child died at birth. Akhenaten had fathered six children, but he had no son and heir.

The harshness with which society views father-daughter incest and the public indignation which the act arouses when it becomes known have a dual origin. First, it is extremely important for the unity of the family, and therefore, the welfare of the clan or tribe, that the jeolousies and complications that uncontrolled incest might produce be prevented. Secondly, and far more emotional than practical in origin, is the natural and powerful attraction of the father to his daughter and vice versa. This is particularly strong, although fairly harmless, in the Oedipal period, but it becomes resurrected in the early teens when the threat can be actualized and is, therefore, dangerous. When an unacceptable wish or impulse is extremely strong, it is necessary to develop equally strong controls against it. In other words, in order for families to remain intact, the mother must not lose completely the Oedipal battle with her daughter. She might well do so without strong taboos on her side to offset the advantages of her younger and possibly more sexually attractive daughter.

Most clinicians agree that brother-sister incest is far more common than is generally realized by the public. There is an adage in some sections of the United States that states, "A virgin girl over the age of seven is one who can run faster than her brothers." Two other sayings are: "Vice is nice, but incest is best," and "The family that lays together stays together." These adages are only humorous if you accept the fact that they are based upon grains of truth! Brother-sister sexual liaisons rarely come to public attention, and when they do, legal action is taken even more rarely. The lack of social interest in this form of incest, especially when one considers its frequency, must indicate the relatively insignificant role it plays in our culture. These affairs usually are self-limiting, and they do not necessarily impair the future brother-sister relationship. Just how harmful they are to either of the participants has never been assessed fully, but the most damaging aspect undoubtedly is the onus of sin and guilt arbitrarily attached to the act.

Brother-sister sexual play which does not include vaginal penetration is so common as to approach the normal. Most of the truly incestuous relationships are between an older brother and a younger sister by mutual consent. The following vignette illustrates a typical case.

A forty-six-year-old World War II veteran was hospitalized for a severe depression that was a manifestation of manic depressive illness. His forty-year-old sister, sincerely interested in his welfare, volunteered to his therapist that they had experimented with sex, including intercourse, many times when he was in his late teens. She wondered if this early experience had influenced his illness in any way. She was a normal housewife and mother with no history of any emotional instability and with no evidence of any sexual disorders. She was assured that there was no reason to believe that the youthful episodes were related to her brother's illness.

Mother-son incest is noted only for its rarity. Investigations of the few reported cases almost always show that the mother has an emotional disturbance of psychotic depth. The exceptions to this most frequently occur in mental retardation of moderate to severe degree or in other forms of organic brain damage that impair impulse control and the ability to think clearly and adhere to social norms. That many mother-son relationships border on the incestuous has been a literary topic for years, and the role this plays in the emotional disturbance of men is well recognized, but evidence of actual consummation of the act usually is lacking.

One case of mother-son incest became known when the

mother became a patient in a state mental hospital because of some irrational behavior in public. The woman was moderately mentally retarded, and both of her children, a girl fourteen and a boy fifteen, were below normal in intellect. The girl additionally was quite emotionally disturbed and had not attended school, but the boy had managed to get to the fifth grade through the generosity of his teachers. They all slept in the same bed in a disreputable hovel they called home. The father of the children was unknown. The mother had taught her son to have intercourse with her and with his sister whenever he so desired, usually in rotation. According to both mother and son, each female was apt to get jealous of the other if she missed her turn!

This represents an unusual case in which the incest was not a deviation but rather was secondary to more basic psychopathology and mental retardation. Not one of these people was capable of differentiating right from wrong or of exercising control of behavior in keeping with social norms. The mother appeared to have no feeling that her actions had been other than normal.

A similar case, except that it involved grandfather-grandchild incest, came to attention when a pregnant twelve year old was brought to the clinic by her mother. The woman, an illiterate creature from the lowest possible level of poverty, shocked the young intern by exclaiming that she, "knowed that pappy wuz gonna knock up one of the girls if he didn't quit foolin' with 'em."

The irate intern demanded to know why the woman had allowed her father to molest his own granddaughter, but he was completely floored by her answer. "I can't do nothing with him," she said. "If he ain't foolin' with the girls, he's screwin' one of my boys!" The welfare department was called into action! Obviously this woman operated at a level of sophistication that precluded the normal social taboos.

Father-daughter incest receives more medical and legal attention than all other forms of incest combined. There are no accurate figures as to its frequency, but it certainly is far more common than is generally known. Almost every family physician can tell of many cases in his practice that have never come to public or legal attention, and father-daughter seduction is a familiar story to all who do psychotherapy with females. The act is not confined to any particular socioeconomic status, and it is a mistake to consider it a habit restricted to the lower classes. While it is true that legal action for father-daughter incest is taken infrequently among those in the upper socioeconomic groups, this is equally true of all offenses, sexual or otherwise. The psychiatrist or minister is more apt to be involved with the middle or upper classes than is the law.

The strong sexual attraction between father and daughter has necessitated the equally strong taboos against it. Freud and others have spoken eloquently of the Oedipal period and of the normal attraction of the child to the parent of the opposite sex at about ages five to seven. The average boy resolves this Oedipal situation rather completely when he passes beyond this stage by identifying with the father and deciding to get his own "mother" at a future day. He does this because he fears his father's punitive reaction if he pursues his desires in competition with him and because his mother does not encourage his advances. We have discussed the possible dangers of undue maternal encouragement or seduction.

The resolution is far less definitive in the little girl. Both boy and girl children are strongly identified with the mother during the first few years of their lives, but unlike the boy, the girl continues this identification throughout adulthood if she is to be normal. Even under average circumstances her Oedipal attachment to father may not reach full resolution until she is married or even until she has her first child. Only one of these events may terminate her unconscious longing to usurp her mother's position with father and to become father's lover in actuality. An overly seductive father and/or a mother who presents a poor role model may make it difficult or impossible for the daughter to achieve the normal resolution. This may result in several possible difficulties, but the incestuous yearnings usually are confined to fantasy or to symbiotic acting-out as is seen in the May-December marriages or even in promiscuous sexual activity.

The universality and the frequency of father-daughter incest make it difficult to stereotype, but the following cases are fairly representative of types from two differing socioeconomic levels.

Miss Blackwell confessed her incestuous relationship with her father to her family physician when she was receiving a routine physical examination prior to entering college. She had become guilt-ridden about the relationship and felt that she must confide in someone. A secondary reason for the confession was that she felt that her leaving for college would place the sexual burden upon her younger sister. She told that she had been having frequent sexual relations with her father since about age ten but stated that she only recently had begun to feel that it was wrong. Her negative feelings had been intensified by her father's unreasonable jealousy and his refusal to allow her to have dates or to be alone with any boy of her own age. She felt that she was being allowed to go to college only because the younger sister would be taking her place. One can only speculate upon whether or not she felt some unconscious jealousy over the possibility of being replaced by her sister.

Miss Blackwell was the oldest of four children. Her father was a rather prominent farmer who also did parttime ministerial work in a very fundamental church. He was a respected and honored figure in a rural area of the southwest where even itinerate ministers are held in some awe. Her mother was a rather sickly and complaining person who had given over the care of the household little by little to the oldest daughter by the time she was nine or ten years of age. The mother was a shadowy personality who seemed to be of little significance in the overall family scheme. It appeared very probable that she had some awareness of the relationship between her daughter and husband but that she had been able to ignore or to deny it or perhaps even to encourage it.

The father and mother came to see the physician upon his request. At first the father denied the entire story and appeared hurt and offended by the accusation, but he quickly agreed with his daughter's statement when the physician threatened to turn the matter over to the law. He made no particular defense for his actions but asked forgiveness and understanding of both his wife and daughter. He assured everyone that it would not happen again and that he had no designs upon the younger girl. The mother did not appear particularly upset and stated that she had been suspicious for some time but that she trusted her family. The interviewing physician felt that she tended to blame the daughter far more than her husband but that she dreaded her departure from the house as it meant that she would now inherit the full role of housewife again. There had been no sexual contact between the husband and wife for over five years.

This case, like most of its kind, was not reported to the law. The physician rightfully felt that nothing could be gained by this and that the family would be totally destroyed by the legal action and resultant publicity. Had it been available to the area, a form of family therapy would have been the logical choice of disposition. One might argue that the family unit already has effectively destroyed, but cases that are reported to the law and do go to court tell a different story. This aspect will be discussed later.

Charlotte came from a very low socioeconomic group, a second generation welfare family. She was first seen in the clinic for persistent enuresis at the age of ten. She was brought for medical attention by a foster mother with whom she had been placed by the welfare department six months previously, after her mother had murdered her father. The examining pediatrician discovered that Charlotte had a marital vaginal entroitus with signs of a healed tear at the vaginal entrance, and because of this he requested a conference with her mother. The mother was then in the county jail awaiting sentencing, but she was being brought to the university clinic for prenatal care every other week and was therefore readily available for interview.

Charlotte's mother obviously was either mentally retarded or a simple schizophrenic or both! She willingly told an incredible story, but one which Charlotte verified completely. She said that Charlotte's father first had intercourse with her when Charlotte was about seven years of age. Since Charlotte had some minor vaginal bleeding, the father had admitted his act. He was not at all remorseful; in fact, he had chided his wife about how much better he liked "young stuff." Neither Charlote nor her mother complained about the situation after that. The incestuous relationship became a frequent affair, never discussed, but accepted as normal.

On the night of his murder, Charlotte's father had begun to make sexual overtures to his wife—a rare act that pleased her even though sex was of no interest to her. He had progressed far enough to arouse her interest somewhat when he suddenly said that he would rather have Charlotte and demanded that his wife go get her from another room. Charlotte was a very sound sleeper; so it was some time before the mother got her awake and brought her back to the husband's bed. By this time he had totally lost interest in both of them, and with some annoyance told them to go back to sleep! The mother became enraged at this dual rejection, grabbed a shotgun which was standing in the corner, and blew his head off! (Parenthetically, the woman was released on bond and became pregnant by her deceased husband's brother on the day of the funeral!)

Fortunately, very few cases end this tragically. One can

only speculate about the future for poor Charlotte, but there is much evidence to indicate that life will be a rocky road for her. This evidence does not clearly answer the question of what happens to the daughter who is a partner to father-daughter incest when it does not end so catastrophically?

The future of the girl may depend almost entirely upon how the incestuous relationship reaches it conclusion. Undoubtedly there are thousands of incidents of incest that come to some sort of natural conclusion that does not involve public knowledge or family confrontation and in which there are no ill effects. There are many others that come to the attention of a psychiatrist, a family physician or a minister accidentally, usually in later life, and in which no ill effects can be shown for certain. It appears that those which are most harmful to the girl are those which end in court and in the punishment of the father and the physical breakdown of the family. In these cases the girl bears a dual burden in that she feels guilty because of the betrayal of her mother and because her father has suffered for something that she feels was equally her fault.

The little girl's guilt stems from her awareness that she was not totally passive in the relationship. She is not only conscious that she has been seductive toward her father but that she has enjoyed the relationship from two aspects. First, she has been pleased by the attention and sexual play. Second, she has enjoyed the supremacy she has gained over her mother. When she sees herself become an object of pity and concern while her father is subjected to humiliation and prison sentence, she cannot help but live under a cloud of guilt and remorse. This is an aspect of father-daughter incest that should receive attention by the authorities and by all who feel particularly vengeful toward the involved man.

The mother of these father-daughter incestuous relationship usually fits the role portrayed in the case examples above. It appears that she unconsciously abdicates her role as wife and encourages the chosen daughter to take her place.

(For example, little Charlotte could cook and sew well by age eight.) She may appear very irate and distraught when faced with the reality of the situation. This reaction is not simulated, but rather it represents a breakdown of her defenses against a conscious awareness of what was happening.

She usually is a woman very insecure in all ways, and she does not conceptualize herself as a sexually attractive person. She rarely enjoys sexual relations except as a means of getting attention. She is willing to trade her superior relationship to the girl for one of equality, or even inferiority, if only she is allowed to avoid the housewifely responsibilities. She either feels neutral toward her daughter, or she feels actual unconscious hostility. Occasionally a true physical disability has necessitated the woman's abdication, but this is the exception rather than the rule.

The mother's role may be more passive in one commonly reported variety of incest; that between stepfather and stepdaughter. Whether or not these cases represent true incestuous relationships is a moot question, but they are legally defined as such. Since there is no actual blood relationship, the internalized prohibiting forces are weakened or absent on both sides. An ambivalent or hostile relationship between mother and daughter, a relationship frequently seen when a mother remarries, may provide the daughter with an excellent motive for seducing the father as a method of getting even with the mother. This type of incest is most commonly seen in girls over the age of puberty, even into the late teens or early twenties. The stepfather may or may not take an active role, and usually he does not know that he is being used as a battleground by his two females, or if he does, he enjoys the spoils of battle.

One twenty-year-old girl who had slept with her stepfather for almost four years came into psychotherapy after a hysterical suicide gesture in which she superficially cut her wrists. She could soon verbalize to her therapist her contempt for her mother, and she became consciously aware that the affair with her stepfather was a way of expressing her negative feelings toward her mother. Not only did she not enjoy the sexual relationship, she actually found it disgusting, and she had resolved unsuccessfully to stop it many, many times. Her feelings arose from a belief that her mother had been responsible for the divorce that had deprived her of her beloved father. She was obtaining revenge by taking away mother's "father!"

The father's role is somewhere between active and passive in most cases of incest. He usually is a weak man who cannot withstand the normal seductions of his daughter. Simultaneously he receives the unconscious message from his wife that she approves of a replacement for her. You will recognize that he has a major item of pedophilia in his makeup and that this sense of inferior masculinity leads him to a partiality for younger females.

Some incestuous fathers seem to show another personality facet—that of a strong, warped sense of possessiveness. They see their family members, especially the females, as objects without personal rights—objects to be manipulated and used as they see fit. They actually are weak men who make themselves feel a sense of masculine superiority by exacting their authority over the relatively defenseless daughter. One can easily see that there is an unconscious hostile component toward females that is very near the surface, even though these men consciously rationalize that they do their daughters no harm.

Incestuous relationships may indicate individual psychopathology, but they invariably indicate a difficulty within the family unit. Frequently they come to light when the girl gets older, is attracted to a male within her peer group, and seeks outside help in breaking off the affair with her father. They also are reported when the girl gets angry with her father for some action that she interprets as a rejection and "tells on him" in retaliation. The adage that "hell hath no fury like a woman scorned" may not appear applicable to father-daughter incest, but many men have learned to their sorrow that a woman is a woman is a woman!

It always is preferable that cases of incest be handled as emotional imbalances within the individuals and the family unit rather than as legal offenses. The tendency to bring vengeance upon the male may not be in the best interests of all concerned, and it may be most injurious to his victim. It appears obvious that much harm may arise from hasty legal action, and it is very difficult to determine how anyone may be helped by making the father a criminal. It may, in some instances, be necessary to remove a child from the home, especially one in the younger age bracket, but if this can be done without criminal charges being filed, all will profit.

12

Madonna-Prostitute Syndrome

THE MADONNA-PROSTITUTE syndrome refers to a condition in which the male unconsciously places females into two diametrically opposing groups: madonnas (symbols of mother) and prostitutes (symbols of evil). This type of man finds it desirable, or in some cases even essential, to consider the woman with whom he interacts sexually as a prostitute or as some degraded woman, since the concept of a sexual activity with a mother figure (madonna) is unacceptable to him. This syndrome is not a diagnostic entity and is not a true sexual deviation. It is included in this category because it represents a relatively severe sexual maldevelopment, components of which can be seen in many of the classical deviations already discussed, and because it tends, in the extreme, to be compulsive and repetitive.

Freud wrote of the "condition of love" that he had observed men to make in their choice of a love object. He wrote: "A virtuous and reputable woman never possesses the charm required to exalt her to an object of love; this attraction is exercised only by one who is more or less sexually discredited, whose fidelity and loyalty admit of some doubt . . . by rough characterization this condition could be called that of a 'love for a harlot'."

Freud was saying that some men are motivated by strong, unconscious factors to choose a debased woman or to degrade the sexual object in some manner. Love to them is something associated with that which is angelic and ethereal (madonnas and mothers), and sex is a part of that which is ugly, animalistic, and primitive. Freud further stated, "When such men love, they have no desire, and when they desire, they cannot love."

A minor degree of this condition cannot always be considered pathological. Many reputable marriage manuals and so-called sexual guides have advised that the successful wife should abandon all inhibitions in the bed chamber. It has been said with some realism that an ideal wife should be "a queen in the parlor, a mother in the kitchen, and a whore in the bedroom." Perhaps no normally adjusted man wants his wife to have an affair with his friend, but, on the other hand, he does like to know that his associates find his wife sexually attractive. Considerable sums of money are invested in clothes and cosmetics to insure this latter point. Much of this is "male ego;" that is, the man simply wants others to admire something he owns, but an underlying part blends imperceptibly into the madonna-prostitute syndrome.

The madonna-prostitute syndrome springs from a situation in which the man has learned to overidealize the mother image and simultaneously to categorize all sexual activities as evil. This type of man is ordinarily the product of a mother who has bound him closely to her but has given him the impression that she still maintains her Victorian virginity. The man has been led to believe, and it has become a deeply imbedded part of his unconscious personality, that all forms of sex are evil and dirty acts. The message becomes so ingrained upon him that he is impotent, at least to some degree, with all "good" women.

A French cartoon published just after World War II showed two women, arms around each other, gazing upward with obvious admiration at a large portrait of a woman. One is saying, "That's my mother . . . a saint. No man ever touched her!" Had the cartoonist let the speaker be a male, he would have been expressing to perfection the unconscious sentiments of the men affected with the madonna-prostitute syndrome.

We have seen that all sexual deviations and associated syndromes occur in varying degrees of complexity and severity. The madonna-prostitute syndrome is no exception. It ranges on a continuum from the normal, of which we have spoken, to the extreme which is exemplified by this most unusual case.

Mrs. MP was a thirty-six-year-old housewife of truly remarkable beauty for any age. The following story was told to her family physician, who promptly referred her for psychiatric consultation. She gave this usual history after having become extremely and justifiably angry at her husband, but even after she had reconciled the differences with him several days later, she did not retract it. He did not deny it when he came for interview, but once the differences were settled between them, neither of them felt that it was worth persuing psychiatrically.

Mr. MP had treated his wife with a chivalry usually reserved for fiction prior to their marriage. He had kissed her many times during a year's courtship, but their premarital lovemaking had not even included any serious "necking," as it was known in those days. She was a very beautiful girl, who, throughout high school and two years of college, had been the object of innumerable sexual advances, all of which she had rebuffed. She was charmed and enchanted by her future husband's genteel and restrained approach to her. Her romantic fantasies came to a shattering conclusion on the night of her wedding.

Mr. MP remained his old chivalrous and genteel self and kissed his wife a platonic goodnight on the first evening of their honeymoon. This continued for over a week of an otherwise ideal relationship. She was sexually inexperienced but not so naive but that she questioned the fact that he did not even get an erection or make the slightest advance toward her. She was beginning to wonder if there was something wrong with her and to feel that she might be to blame for his lack of ardor. However, when she approached him with her doubts and questions on about the eighth postwedding evening, he made a suggestion to her that filled her with dismay.

Mr. MP proposed that they play a game. He asked that his wife go to one of the bars near their honeymoon hotel and make herself available as a pickup. He knew that a woman of her beauty would have no problem picking up a man. Mr. MP would go to a movie so that his wife could bring the man to the room and have sexual intercourse with him. Mrs. MP was to have the man out of the room before midnight, the proposed hour of the husband's return.

Mrs. MP was telling this fantastic story sixteen years after it first began. She could give no credible reason as to why she had complied with this strange wish except to say that she wanted to do anything to please her husband and that she was very ignorant in the ways of the world. She made much of the fact that she was sexually innocent and almost totally lacking in factual knowledge. She remembered that she had been so shocked at the request that she had complied with it in a trance-like condition before realizing what she had done. However that may be, as attractive as she was, she had no difficulty in making a contact and in losing her virginity within the hour.

Mr. MP returned from the movie sometime after his wife's sexual partner had departed. He, upon being told that she had done as he had requested, asked her no questions but immediately began wooing her ardently. As a part of his sexual foreplay, he inserted his tongue into her vagina. He then vigorously consummated his marriage as befitting a young, new husband.

Incredible as this episode may seem, the next sixteen years of this marriage were even more so. For an average of one time per week, and here the reader may wish to make his own mathematical calculations, Mrs. MP went through the same routine at the request of her husband. She would leave the house, have intercourse with some man, return to have Mr. MP check her vagina with his tongue, then they would engage in mutually satisfactory sexual relations. Three children were born during these years, and due to this rather bizarre sexual life, the parentage of these children was obviously questionable, although that subject was never discussed or even mentioned by either of them.

Mr. MP occasionally accused his wife of untruthfulness and of not having made a sexual contact as she stated. It appeared that he could not get an erection and have intercourse unless he tasted semen in her vagina! Some of her sexual contacts apparently had not been able to ejaculate, and since she was not always aware of this, she had been unjustly accused of not cooperating upon some occasions. Sometimes the husband insisted that she go back for another trial, but at others he would be generous with her and forget the whole thing for that night.

This was not a couple of outlandish eccentrics living an antisocial existence. They were middle class citizens in a respectable suburban neighborhood, and Mr. MP was a successful businessman in real estate. They were churchgoers and civic leaders in their community, and not one of their close associates or neighbors apparently suspected the bizarre way of life they practiced. It had taken ingenuity to continue this habit year after year, but the sexual attractiveness and the intelligence of Mrs. MP had been a valuable asset. Most of her contacts were traveling men, and she attempted never to have the same man twice, although this had not been possible 100 percent of the time. She became quite angry when asked if she had ever charged them or accepted favors from them. She also denied ever receiving any pleasure from the act. It was as if either charging or enjoying would have made the act immoral or unacceptable to her.

This couple would not hear of a complete psychiatric evaluation, and they never returned to the physician to whom Mrs. MP first made the confessions, despite the fact that he had been their family doctor for fifteen years. The sexual pathology of Mr. MP appears rather certain, but what is one to make of the wife who agrees to this sort of life style without major objection? Mrs. MP's explanation that she was willing to cooperate in order to please her husband and to retain his affection sounds a bit too reasonable and glib on the surface. An activity this divergent from the norm must be motivated by a rather deepseated personality deficit which, in the case of Mrs. MP, we had no opportunity to evaluate. We can speculate that she also needed to degrade herself before being able to be a "normal" wife.

There are many unusual aspects to the case of the MP's. One of these is that Mr. MP made no sexual advances toward his wife prior to marriage. The man afflicted with this syndrome sometimes will attempt to have premarital intercourse in order to convince himself that the girl actually is "the prostitute" to whom he can relate. This type of man may be a regular sexual athlete for a long period of time prior to the wedding and then find himself suddenly impotent thereafter. The mere legalization and aura of respectability that the marriage rite confers is enough to place the girl who was a sexual object a few days before into the category of madonna and, therefore, unapproachable.

The female counterpart of this syndrome sometimes accounts for multiple marriages. These women may be totally frigid with their husbands but discover by experimentation that they are "turned on" and have orgasms when engaging in intercourse with another person. They may divorce the husband, marry the newfound lover, but then find that they are frigid with the new husband after the relationship has been legalized. One such woman was on her fifth marriage before it dawned upon her that there was a marked neurotic repetition to her way of life and that she should seek help.

Another young wife sought help after three years of marriage to a devoted husband. She had been a virgin at marriage, and although she had fantasized great things about married life, nothing came of it. She did not become erotically aroused even slightly, and intercourse more and more became a dreaded ordeal with real vaginal pain.

They had done extensive petting prior to marriage, and she always had become aroused and felt that she had come near to orgasm. Marriage destroyed even that bit of excitement and pleasure for her. And then she made a discovery by doing a thing totally foreign and even repugnant to her. She seduced and had intercourse with a laboring man working near her house! She did not have an orgasm, but she became mildly aroused. She repeated the act with many different men over the next few months but made no attachment to any of them. She enjoyed every single time with these men, but try as she would, she could not even feign arousal with her husband. She was an intelligent and well-read woman who realized that something was wrong with her. This knowledge, plus a growing sense of guilt and shame (and parenthetically a fear of venereal disease), drove her to seek treatment which continues at this time.

The madonna-prostitute syndrome has produced a great disappointment for some young brides who could not have anticipated what was going to happen to them. One such girl came for psychiatric consultation about one year after her marriage to an all-American football player at a major university. They had had premarital intercourse only once, and that was about a week before the wedding. She was a virgin, and he was sexually inexperienced, so the attempts at intercourse were not very successful, but not because of his inability to become aroused. However, he was able to maintain an erection only long enough to complete a few seconds of intercourse. His erection usually subsided the moment he began to make the insertion. She came to the consultation after confiding in her minister, but when asked to bring her husband with her for the next visit, she said that she did not think that he would come. She had approached this with him upon several occasions, but he always got extremely angry and accused her of being "oversexed." She was correct; he did not come.

There appeared to be little reason to treat the young wife psychiatrically since she had no real symptoms or discomfort not connected with her husband. His refusal to seek help could have indicated that he was not basically unhappy with his condition, but more likely it meant that he was not able to face the fact that he was not the "man" that his football history indicated that he should have been. He had not made it into the professional ranks, and now that his athletic career was over, he had nothing substantial to support his ego.

A similar case involved an athlete whose pathology was much more severe. He requested that his young wife have intercourse with a friend and became quite "sulky" when she flatly refused. He settled the issue a few days later by bringing his friend home for a few drinks and then forcibly restraining his wife while his friend raped her. He became irate when she confessed the incident to a psychiatrist who requested to see him. He went for one interview reluctantly but refused to return. This couple eventually divorced, but the husband never understood why his wife was upset over such a trifle. She continued in psychotherapy, not because of any trauma connected with the experience, but rather in order to work out her feelings about her ex-husband and to understand why she actually had enjoyed the act while being disgusted with herself at the same time!

Many men with this syndrome are like this young athlete. They can remain potent only if their wives will have intercourse with another man and allow them to observe. Some men have carried this to the point of enticing or even hiring other men to sleep with their wives while they observe, with or without their wives' consent. There are a surprising number of known cases in which the wife has freely cooperated, and many more of these probably never come to medical attention. When cases do come to light, the women usually say that they have been coerced into the act against their will or that they are willing to "sacrifice" for their husbands' happiness.

One case had a minor variation to it. The man in this marriage was relatively potent, and by that I mean that he was able to have intercourse an average of once every six to eight weeks. Even this seemed to be dependent upon how cooperative his wife was, however. He not only requested that she have intercourse with another man while he watched; he requested that it be with a black man. The significance of this takes on greater meaning when it is known that this Caucasian man was extremely prejudiced toward minority groups. This, to his warped unconscious, was even further degration and gave the act a greater value to him. At the same time, he was able to identify with the black man who, he felt, was sexually superior. He believed that men of the Negro race possessed larger genitalia and that they were better able to satisfy women.

This story came to light when the wife entered psychiatric treatment for a middle-aged depression. She expressed great feelings of worthlessness and guilt over her past sexual behavior, and these feelings were even greater because she confessed that she had enjoyed these many occasions. She simultaneously had experienced each of the sexual sessions as punitive and degrading, but since she had no respect for herself or for her husband, she felt that each of them deserved to be punished in this humiliating manner. It seemed that these sexualized acts of atonement had functioned to prevent her from becoming clinically depressed for many years. This highly aberrant behavior had acted as a defense against depression, but since it was a neurotic and unhealthy defense, it eventually failed. The husband denied the story and maintained that it was product of his wife's deranged mind, but even after she had recovered completely, she insisted that it was true, and there were many reasons to believe her. Whether or not she returned to her past way of life is unknown.

One interesting variant of the madonna-prostitute syndrome does not appear until after a man's wife has her first baby. This man may have maintained a normal sex life for several years only to find that he no longer can be aroused sexually by his wife once she has become a mother. Erections are no problem with other women, and he may be shocked and despondent over his lack of feeling for a woman to whom he was greatly attached a few weeks previously.

An example of the postdelivery development of this syndrome was referred for consultation by the woman's obstetrician about five months after the birth of the couple's first child. They were an attractive, intelligent, and well-motivated couple in their mid-twenties. They were very much in love; the pregnancy was planned; and they had the healthy male child they both desired. They saw themselves as a very fortunate and happy couple with a wonderful life ahead of them. The first hint of trouble appeared when the young mother returned from her six weeks' checkup and told her husband that the doctor had said that sexual intercourse could be resumed. She had expected a gala evening after the many weeks of forced abstinence, but he had a very logical reason for postponing it. Days passed into weeks, and he began to run out of plausible excuses. Her first thought was that he had found a substitute for her during the "dry spell," but she could not believe that this was actually so. She was hurt and angry at what she perceived to be a rejection of herself. She bluntly confronted him with her fantasy of his infidelity. He denied it adamantly; then in tears he told her that he still loved her but that he had absolutely no sexual feeling for her. Neither could understand what had happened.

It takes no genius to comprehend the magnitude of the

tragedy that had befallen this young couple. Fortunately, they were intelligent people, and they loved each other. They went to her obstetrician and explained the situation, and he, having previously experienced this sort of a situation in his practice, referred them for psychiatric consultation. Each was interviewed separately; then they were seen together. They were basically a very stable and mature couple with this one minor exception on his part. It was decided that they would be seen in joint therapy unless either of them wanted a solo session. Neither of them ever asked for a visit alone, and sexual relations were returning to normal after a few weeks' therapy. It appears obvious that a case like this has a better outlook than those previously discussed since the syndrome did not come to the surface until the wife actually had become a mother. This meant that it was of a far lesser degree of severity in this man than in the case of Mr. MP.

Couples may play many games with each other when one or both has a problem in the madonna-prostitute realm. One sees wives who cannot bring themselves to cooperate fully but who desire to retain their mate's attention. They may concoct situations in which suspicions of their infidelity are so great as to satisfy the husband's needs yet in which they remain totally innocent. One such case was Gloria.

Gloria was in psychotherapy at the request of one of her teachers who felt that emotional blocks prevented her from achieving her full potential. She was a twenty-four-year-old postgraduate student in art. She was married to a postgraduate student in one of the hard sciences at the same university. Her husband always had been unreasonably jealous of her, but Gloria took this as a form of flattery and was undisturbed by it. Gradually she noted that their sexual contacts never occurred except after a severe argument, and that all the arguments involved false accusations of her relations with other men.

Gloria liked sex. The infrequent contacts with her

husband were not enough for her; yet she could not bring herself to have an affair, even though she had thought seriously of it and had plenty of opportunities. She compromised. She began to set up situations that produced suspicions. She became adept at making it appear that she was involved with other men and equally adept at making it look as if she were trying to keep it a secret. But somehow her husband always found out about it! This would be followed by accusations, recriminations, and threats, but understanding and forgiveness quickly replaced the negative feelings and led directly into a sexual orgy very gratifying to both. This sexual activity would continue for three to six weeks, gradually declining, then Gloria would start planning another spurious affair.

There have been glimpses of the madonna-prostitute syndrome in many of the other chapters of this book. The critical reader must remember that it not only occurs in a disguised form in some of the sexual deviations, but that it also can be observed in conventional society. The modern-day monstrosity, the cocktail party, performs an excellent laboratory in which to observe husbands subtly encouraging their wives to have affairs and also encouraging friends and acquaintances to take advantage of the offer. The husband rarely is consciously aware of this, and only an observer trained in psychiatric techniques may detect it. This same husband, if the syndrome exists only in latent form, may become extremely wrathful if he discovers that his wife has been unfaithful to him. The wife of this sort of man may know this intuitively, and by making it impossible for the husband not to find out about her affairs, purposefully may invoke his wrath and express her hostility toward him.

It is easy to see the number of "games" made possible by variations of this syndrome. Marriage counselors, family therapists, and ministers probably see more of them than do physicians, but even the casual observer can watch the unconscious moves in everyday social interaction. It may sound facetious to refer to a sometimes distressing situation as a game, but many couples make just that of the minor variations of this interesting syndrome.

The game requires a third participant in most instances. The social milieu is filled with men who are adept, perhaps without knowing it, at picking up cues from those couples involved in the game. These men are quite available to "help," and many feel themselves successful seducers without ever knowing that a complete interaction has gone on at an unconscious level and that they are the unimportant pawns in it.

The syndrome, at some level, is far more common than is generally thought. It is understandable that most people are reluctant to speak of it even to a physician. It is very rare for the man involved to seek help or to even question his actions. Most cases come to light when the wife becomes angry over some unrelated event or when she, for some reason, begins to question her own role.

Many women do not cooperate with husbands who suffer from this syndrome. The wife of a prominent physician asked for advice about her husband's problem. He had begun hinting to her that she should have a boyfriend after two years of near perfect marriage. She refused to take this seriously until he became more and more insistent. Thinking that he was having an affair and was trying to make his own actions justified, she hired a private detective. This proved only one thing—that he was totally without outside interests. She then confessed her suspicions to him and told him about hiring the private investigator. He was amused by her worry and assured her that he loved her as much as ever but that he could love her more if only she would do as he requested.

The woman could not bring herself to cooperate, and since her husband became enraged at the suggestion that he see a psychiatrist, she filed for a divorce.

The only logical treatment is analytical psychotherapy

to produce a higher level of psychosexual maturity. The difficulty lies in getting the man to accept the treatment. He usually is comfortable with his life so long as the wife cooperates, and as stated, he rarely volunteers for something that he does not feel he needs. Perhaps the newer innovation, Swinging (chapter fourteen), will solve the problem since it is a form of ritualization and organization of the madonna-prostitute syndrome.

13

Prostitution

PROSTITUTION IS ENGAGEMENT in a sexual relationship purely for financial gain. It does not represent a true sexual deviation in most cases. It may be a simple expedient for earning money; the symptom of a mental derangement or of a character disorder; or it may be the result of actual deviation in the development of sexuality. Only in this latter sense is it a sexual deviation, but we will discuss it as such since our society ordinarily considers it an unacceptable sexual practice—at least on the overt level. We will see that modern prostitution relates directly to some forms of male sexual deviation.

Perhaps there is no better statement about prostitution than the one by Polly Adler in her book, *A House Is Not A Home*. She said, "Many of my customers never seemed to realize that a prostitute is just as much a product of our so-called culture as is a college professor or a bootblack and, as with them, her choice of occupation has been dictated by environmental and personality factors. No woman is born a whore and any woman may become one."

The statement, "No woman is born a whore and any woman may become one," was said in a more melodious fashion by Rudyard Kipling in one of his poems, ". . . and the Colonel's lady and Judy O'Grady are sisters under the skin."

We will not speak of the many mistresses, or "kept" women, who do not make a cash transaction but who just as surely exchange their affections for some form of material gain. The subtle difference lies in the feeling of the woman for the man and in her commitment to him. Theoretically the prostitute invests nothing but a limited amount of time and the temporary use of her body in several relationships; whereas the mistress is expected to be emotionally involved in an ongoing relationship with a single paramour.

The *Kama Sutra* says, "There are women who search for love, and there are those who search for money." That statement of centuries ago remains perfectly true today. The ancient philosopher intended to indicate that only those women who search for money should be considered prostitutes, but the fact is that an aberrant search for love may motivate female prostitution as well as the search for financial gain.

The history of prostitution is such that it has been called the oldest profession in the world. This may be an exaggeration, but there is evidence that it has presented difficulties in many societies because of the mixed feelings and attitudes toward it. Certainly it must have been a problem of long standing when Jesus Christ spoke to the Scribes and Pharisees and advised only those who were without sin to cast the first stone at the prostitute. Society's feelings and attitudes have changed very little in the past two thousand years despite the so-called sexual revolution and the age of sexual enlightenment. We still do not know whether to stone the prostitute or to pray for her, so we usually soothe our consciences and settle the issue by doing both.

The origin of prostitution is lost in antiquity, but logical inferences can be made. It probably began not with the woman selling her body to a man for sexual use, but with one man selling or renting a woman he possessed to another. This appears plausible since women were the chattel of men for the first several centuries of mankind's history, and they were bought and sold as any other piece of property in many societies until quite recently. Prostitution as we know it could not have existed until there was a certain degree of female freedom, because a woman could not sell or lease herself until she possessed herself!

Prostitution obviously could not have existed as an ubiquitous institution for so many centuries unless there was a demand for it. No matter how strong the motivation or how intense the drive from the female side, the existence of the practice of prostitution, as in any business, depended upon paying customers. A discussion of the institution requires a look at the men who make it possible and who have kept it going.

The primary reason for a male's visit to a prostitute has changed somewhat with time as we shall see later, but it began as a simple desire for sexual intercourse. With a wife or lover, at least until recent times, sexual intercourse always entailed a risk of pregnancy and the responsibilities that followed it. There was no such feeling of responsibility with a prostitute and no need to fear embarrassing social and legal entanglements. Then, as today, the prostitute offered uncomplicated sexual pleasure with no investment other than a small sum of money.

Another possible motivation for the man's visit to a prostitute is the belief that has long been held, whether truth or fiction, that she is a true expert in sex. The customer could expect much more from the expert than from his wife or a paramour. Some women did become experts in the art of pleasing men, but this included much more than the sexual act itself. Many societies trained young girls in the exacting art of gratifying the male, and in some of them it became an honored and well-rewarded profession. It is not the sexual act itself that is most important in male gratification. It is, as all experts have learned, first essential to bolster the man's ego. He must be made to feel a "real man." The true professionals learned the little ways and words that made a man think that he was just a little better than anyone else. The girls even learned to feign orgasm and to do this rather quickly with a paying customer, especially in those houses which depended upon a rapid turnover. Shortening the length of stay with each individual increased the number of customers who could be served per unit of time.

A third reason for visiting a prostitute is more consistent and obvious. Men away from home—sailors, military men, travelers of various types—frequently lack the time to make the contacts needed to develop nonprofessional feminine relationships, and in many instances the women simply would not be available for that sort of companionship. They seek sexual entertainment that is readily and easily available with a minimum of complication and personal investment. The thriving centers of prostitution traditionally have been those areas frequented by a transient male population. That a man will do things away from home that he hardly dares fantasize otherwise is a well-known phenomenon capitalized upon by many prostitutes. Convention centers that host large meetings of men are fertile hunting grounds for today's "women of the night."

There appeared to be an upsurge of prostitution during the Victorian period of history. A man of this puritanical age might have been motivated to visit a prostitute in order to have some relaxed sexual pleasure with a woman who did not feel that it was utterly sinful or that she was being a sacrificial lamb. The man, no less than the woman, probably believed sincerely that it was not possible for his wife, presumably a decent woman, to enjoy the sexual act. He might even have visited the prostitute out of a feeling of altruism for his wife; that is, a desire to relieve her of a burdensome and unpleasant task. No doubt many wives of all periods of history have concurred in this and have by sundry means encouraged their husbands to look elsewhere for sexual gratification.

A last speculation in this vein concerns a long and deeply held belief that sexual abstinence is harmful to the male. The idea that a man's good health depends upon regular sexual intercourse has remained viable into this century. Whether or not this concept merely represents the male's rationalization of his actions and impulses is a moot question, but it certainly has helped him to accept the idea of paying for sex while maintaining his own self-esteem and feeling of worth. The deeply ingrained idea of a double standard allowed him to visit prostitutes while condemning sexuality among his own female relations or for his girl friend.

We have listed some relatively normal reasons for the support of prostitution from the male viewpoint. This is not to imply that these reasons are openly acceptable to society, but rather that the pathological factor is minimal or absent. Of the following two reasons, the first borders upon the pathological, and the second definitely represents an abnormality.

Some men visit prostitutes because they actually are, or they feel themselves to be, so unattractive as to exclude close relationships with a normal woman. This varies from simple shyness and timidity to overt physical deformity. In either instance, the male feels unable to obtain sexual gratification except when it is a business arrangement. At one time this was also true of the very young and inexperienced male who might even be encouraged to visit a prostitute by his father in order that he might learn the details of sexual life from a professional teacher. Apparently embarrassment and shame did not enter the picture when the girl was being paid, and a prostitute could never look down upon anyone else for any reason since she usually has occupied a low rung on the social ladder.

There are those cases of men who are relatively or even totally impotent with all females who are conceptualized as "good." This condition, the madonna-prostitute syndrome, as discussed in a previous chapter, prevents a man from having sexual relations with a "good" woman who represents mother. Sex is an evil and sinful thing that can be related only to the prostitute, who is seen as a degraded woman. As Freud said, "Where they love they can feel no passion, and where they feel passion they cannot love." Rather than degrade the woman they love, these men may restrict their sexual activities to prostitutes and either remain single or marry women who make no sexual demands upon them or, in some cases, marry the prostitute.

There is another and still more pathological reason for visiting a prostitute, but this will be discussed later.

And what are the prostitute's reasons? We have intimated that they concern either a search for love or a search for money. Some believe that a third factor is self-evident—sinful depravity or mental illness. We will leave the question of sin to the ministers, but it is just as illogical to assume that all prostitutes are mentally ill women as it is to assume that none of them has an emotional disorder. We always have been a bit too prone to condemn as mentally ill those who do not conform to the dictates of society's sometimes overwhelming conscience. And yet there does seem to be something a little sick about seeking love through prostitution. Frequently these are women who are either borderline in intelligence or have emotional disorders which prevent them from having normal interpersonal relationships. They, like some of their customers, are incapable of relating to the opposite sex on any other level. They are able to delude themselves into a feeling of being wanted and loved—something needed by every human being. Some of these girls have the fantasy that a rich and charming man is going to fall madly in love with them and take them away from it all. This probably happens just often enough to keep the fantasies alive!

The financial motivation in prostitution remains the most significant one by far. For many years, in fact until very recent times, the woman forced to earn her own living was in bad trouble. It was difficult for the educated woman; it was virtually impossible for the uneducated one to survive alone. Many attractive young girls found that they could make more in one evening of prostitution than in a week's work as a waitress or as a domestic worker. Even the few available factory jobs paid miserably low wages for long hours of slave-like labor in horrible surroundings. Many of the short stories and novels of the late 1800's and early 1900's were about the young and innocent country girl who, for a variety of reasons, found herself alone and hungry in the large city. Some lecherous person took advantage of her and left her a ruined and disgraced woman, and she was forced by financial necessity into a life of prostitution. These stories may have been fictional, but like most fiction they were based upon a grain of truth. Many young girls came to the big city seeking their fortunes only to find that they had only one commodity that was marketable—their bodies. When it came to a choice between starvation and prostitution, most of them probably chose to eat.

Recent publicity on drug abuse has pointed out that the enormous expense of supporting a heroin habit usually necessitates illegal methods. The male has several avenues open to him for making enough money to support a heroin habit, but the female is limited largely to prostitution. Beverly, a rather typical example, supported herself and her boyfriend in a moderate addiction by prostitution. The usual expense was about $30 a day (six $5 bags) for both of them. An attractive nineteen-year-old with the face and body of a high school cheerleader had no trouble making this much money in a few hours around New York hotels. She learned to approach men who appeared to be in their forties, rather than the younger, less affluent ones.

Beverly was the daughter of a successful lawyer in an eastern community. She began nonnarcotic drug use in high school, but took her first "snort" of heroin shortly after she entered college. She rarely attended classes after that and had soon spent off her money on drugs. The college dismissed her, but no one could convince Beverly to get help. Her parents became completely discouraged and disowned her once they found that she was supporting a man and herself by prostitution. Beverly eventually came to treatment for gonorrhea contracted through her "business," but she was not interested in changing her way of living.

Before going further into some variations on prostitution as it has developed in recent years, let us take a look at the individual and sociological differences seen in the types of prostitutes. There is extensive overlapping, but we can speak fairly generally of four types. the streetwalker, the house girl, the call girl, and the part-time prostitute.

The streetwalker is that poor creature generally stereotyped as the "whore." She occupies the lowest rung of the prostitute's professional ladder, and of the four types, she is far more apt to be emotionally disturbed or intellectually deficient. She hangs around bars and other places where men congregate in hopes of making a pickup or, as the name implies, she patrols the streets in an undisguised search for customers. Since she is not apt to be a raving beauty, her business is aided by some degree of intoxication in her prospective customers. She usually charges whatever the traffic will bear and operates out of her own room or shabby apartment or depends upon the man to furnish the place of business.

Most major cities have tried to eliminate the street girls. Many of them once had their own territories, usually one or more blocks, which they guarded vigorously. Visitors to San Juan, Puerto Rico, a few years ago could observe frequent disputes between girls who felt that their territory was being infringed upon by a competitor. In some areas a man rarely walked a block without having a proposition from at least one streetwalker. They varied from the attractive beginner to the pathetic aging woman whose time was running out, but the majority of them were in the latter category.

The house girl also is a vanishing breed, at least in this country. The old "cat houses," "red light districts," and more elaborate places run by Madams of notoriety are almost ancient history. It is estimated that one or two houses still exist in each major city, but no true "district" remains. The original logic for confining prostitution to certain areas of a city was that it could thereby be controlled much more efficiently. Periodic examinations of the girls would prevent the spread of venereal disease, and having prostitution in the open would prevent the robbing and blackmailing of customers. Just how well either of these problems was controlled is a question unanswerable and still debated heatedly.

The house girl usually worked on a percentage basis. For each customer she collected a certain sum, and if she failed to meet a quota set by the Madam, her percentage of the take decreased. For example, she might get 50 percent of the take, but only when the total for the day exceeded, let us say, $25. For this she got a place to work, protection from the law, and frequently a home better than she had known previously. Since each girl usually had a set fee, a quick turnover of visitors was desirable. A customer who dallied too long might be charged overtime!

These houses of prostitution, or in more acceptable terms, houses of entertainment, frequently were elaborate and of great reknown. All varieties of entertainment were offered, but the main course was sex with a capital S. The clients came in many varieties from the lonely traveling man to the jaded lothario who could no longer attract women on his own merits. One house in Chicago advertised that it offered something for all males from junior to grandfather, but it left the specifics to the imagination.

The call girl is higher on the socio-economic ladder and is not apt to be overtly emotionally ill, mentally deficient, or forced into the work for economic reasons alone. She may, in fact, be intelligent and capable of being a delightful companion to her customers. Many men may hire her more for this aspect of her trade than for the purely sexual one, and unless she possesses something more than sexual attractiveness, her return business and referrals will be limited.

Call girls operate in a variety of ways. Many may choose their customers with care and accept only those referred from well-known sources. The charge may be up to several hundred dollars per night depending upon the cusomer, the girl, and the situation. Some have pimps who make the contacts for them and who extract fairly large percentages, almost as if they were legitimate business agents. The pimp may or may not be the girl's lover, and he frequently has a "stable" of girls working for him. The nature of her work usually makes a respectable apartment or room a necessary part of the call girl's armamentarium, although some depend upon the customer to furnish this.

Select call girls may make a considerable sum of money. One girl, twenty-six years of age, worked as a secretary for a respected New York City firm. Her salary paid her living expenses quite adequately. However, she worked on weekends as a call girl, taking only customers referred from previously satisfied clients. She did not have a pimp and had operated independently for three years. Occasionally she would take a customer (turn a trick) during the week, but month in and month out she averaged about one and one-half clients per weekend. She charged a flat $100 fee, which meant $600 of extra income per month. It was not required, but she usually expected and received dinner at one of the more expensive restaurants, and sometimes even a Broadway show. This extra money, obviously not reported as income and therefore tax free, was being stored away for the day when she intended to spend a number of leisure years traveling through Europe.

This girl saw herself as an independent business woman.

She was particular about her clients, and she would do nothing except straight sexual intercourse. She protected herself from venereal disease by frequent checkups and from pregnancy by birth control pills. In her three years of work, she had had no difficulty of any kind. She operated so discreetly that she did not pay for police protection. She occasionally had regular dates with men her own age, quite platonic, but had no real romantic interests. She did not enjoy sexual intercourse, nor did she particularly abhor it; she simply viewed it as work for which she was well paid.

The fourth type, the part-time prostitute, is seen manily in resort and tourist areas, although there have been recent reports of "normal" housewives from suburbia engaging in the work in some metropolitan areas. The part-time girl does not depend upon prostitution for a living, and she does not consider it as a regular job. Unlike the girl discussed above, she practices it only sporadically. As a matter of fact, she usually does not class herself as a prostitute at all. Most often she will have some special reason for needing the added income, but occasionally she will admit that it is just a lark for interest's sake alone; an attempt to add some excitement to an otherwise dull existence.

An example of the part-time prostitute is a very attractive young nurse who enjoys a two-to-three week vacation at a very expensive beach resort area each year. She wears expensive clothing and spends quite lavishly during this period of time; a thing she could not possibly afford on her routine income. She "allows" herself to be picked up on the beach, in the lobby, or in the bar of the area chosen, but once she has a customer fairly well on the hook, she explains that it is a business deal with her. Her charm and attractiveness have, for at least four consecutive years, afforded her a very excellent vacation plus a little money for the return trip even though her charge never exceeds $50. She, unlike many other types, also expects to be wined and dined in good style if she has an evening date.

The prostitute has been described by many people as having a high level of identity problems. She tends to see herself as two people: saint and sinner, and as Kipling said of East and West, "never the twain shall meet." The prostitute part of her is the "not-me" sinner, and the other is the "me" that may be a shy, easily embarrassed, almost puritanical female who blushes at an off-color joke in public. This sort of identity split allows some prostitutes to be totally uninhibited and without any standards of conduct on the job, and yet to be highly moralistic people in their social lives. One such girl came to psychiatric treatment with a depression that occurred after her aunt, a beloved person to her, had accidentally learned of her profession. This girl had slept with hundreds of men and had performed every conceivable sexual act for money. The boy whom she dated, a college student in a nearby city, had never been allowed to touch her beyond the petting stage, and she was certain that he thought that she was a virgin. It was not that she found him sexually unattractive, it was that she could not bring herself to behave so wantonly with someone she liked and respected. As this attitude tells us, she had the utmost contempt and disgust for her customers.

What has happened to prostitution as a result of the so-called sexual revolution of the past few years? As one prostitute stated, "Times are damned hard because the amateurs are ruining the business." Others have said, "Why should a man pay for what is being given away?" There is some truth in both of these statements, but as enterprising business people have done for years, many prostitutes have continued to make a living by adapting themselves to the changing times. The major change is that straight sexual intercourse has become a smaller and smaller part of the prostitute's business, and more and more she deals with aberrant sexual practices. And so we come to the most pathological of the reasons for men visiting prostitutes.

The sexual deviant often is forced into a position of

seeking professional companionship because it is so difficult for him to find partners who will cooperate with him in her preferred sexual acts. And so it is that the more aberrant sexual practices have steadily risen in frequency among the prostitute's customers. Such practices as coprophilia and urolagnia (Chapter 15) rarely meet with favor in the average wife or girl friend who finds them disgusting, or at best, ludicrous. A man who would never ask his wife or girl friend to cooperate in such practices may not hesitate to proposition a prostitute. Some girls in large cities tell of customers who have standing appointments. For example, one girl told of a middle-aged man, well dressed and apparently well educated, who regularly paid her $25 every other week for a few minutes of her time. He merely sat in her bathroom, watched her have a bowel movement, paid his $25 and departed.

Prostitutes are asked to perform every sexual act that the most vivid imagination can conceptualize. Most of their customers remain anonymous for obvious reasons, but many are "regulars" as discussed above. Some girls specialize in certain acts and advertise their expertise. For example, one large and somewhat aging practitioner boasted that she had the "biggest and roughest" tongue in the business. Her specialty was "Around the World"—a complete tongue job somewhat similar to a cat bathing a kitten, "guaranteed to produce a bone-breaking orgasm in a mummy!" Modesty never gained a fair lady new customers!

We have discussed prostitution as if it were confined to the heterosexuals, and as if it were a female profession. Male homosexual prostitution, as far as we know, is just as ancient as the female heterosexual variety. Young boys have been raised to be professional prostitutes in almost every civilization on record. In areas of the East, especially during one period in China, the training of boys to become homosexual prostitutes was very elaborate and precise. They were among the most cultured of people for that era, or perhaps for any time in history. Poorer families considered it an honor and a privilege to have their son accepted into this profession; one which almost always insured a comfortable, safe life at a time when that was the privilege of a chosen few.

While heterosexual prostitution appears to be a declining business in this country, homosexual prostitution is felt to be on the upturn throughout the world. There are some few male houses of prostitution, but probably 95 percent of this work is done in solo fashion on street corners, in gay bars, all-night theaters, etc. The male prostitute almost always is under twenty-five years of age, and quite frequently he would be very incensed to be called a homosexual or a prostitute at all. He will argue that he is heterosexual and that he is merely working the "queers" for their money. He will protest a great revulsion for the "queers" and will justify his act as a legitimate business. There is good season to believe that this man may be the customer of the future!

The homosexual prostitute's customers frequently are considerably older—those no longer able to attract men on their own merits. The charge may be from two to five, seldom more than ten dollars, and the act can vary from simple masturbation to fellatio. A cheap hotel room, or even a public bathroom, may be the place of the liaison. An observant eye around 42nd Street and Broadway in New York City will show several young homosexual prostitutes "hustling" at almost any time of the day or night. One young man said that he had no problem earning $50 an evening whenever he wished.

The increase in narcotics use is one motivation behind the increase in homosexual prostitution. An eighteen-year-old needing five dollars for a bag of heroin can always pick up the money in a few minutes by performing fellatio on an older homosexual male. The young addict will swear adamantly that he is not homosexual and that it is merely a method of making money. This may be true, but one must remember that heroin addiction is in itself a method of denial of heterosexuality.

No discussion of prostitution can omit the question of its legal status. Throughout history there have been periodic attempts to eradicate the practice, but all have failed miserably. Most cities no longer have legalized prostitution, the old red light areas are gone, and many authorities believe that the recent increase in syphilis and gonorrhea are partially due to this. When Italy outlawed legal prostitution a few years ago, there was almost immediately a 100 percent increase in the reported cases of venereal disease. However, it cannot be proven with certainly that the increase was due to the changed legal status of prostitution. Regardless of the public health aspect, the legislation of morals and standards of behavior simply cannot work, and a more reasonable approach might be to regulate sensibly some of the practices which are going to exist in spite of all pressures, or failing that, to ignore them.

Another evil secondary to outlawing prostitution is the corruption that invariably occurs in the legal system. Prostitution usually continues to exist in all its forms, but protection money becomes essential. The many side effects from this include increasing the customer's expenditures, decreasing the girl's wages, and increasing the temptation of bribery to the police officials. All in all, there seems little evidence that legislation against prostitution is of value, but that the social changes are doing what the law could not. Women can earn a living at many trades and in all areas of the country. Men can find sexual contacts without restorting to the professional. The motivation to enter prostitution, with the possible exclusion of homosexual prostitution, has decreased simultaneously with a drop in the demand. Could it be that the oldest profession is dying because the world no longer needs it?

14

Group Sex

GROUP SEX IS known as "swinging" by its participants. It refers to sexual activities involving three or more people simultaneously, and it infers an absence of force or coercion. The many possible variations make a more precise definition impossible.

Group sex is listed officially as a sexual deviation in the American Handbook of Psychiatry, but many people, especially those participating in group sex, would object strongly to this categorization. In all fairness, it must be understood that the American Handbook is referring to a variation of group sex, more properly called "gang sex," which includes the element of force and which would exclude the people presently involved in the activity we will describe. Perhaps it is more accurate to call the phenomenon of swinging a social deviation, since many of the participants apparently do not demonstrate the deep-seated personality disorders so commonly seen in the true sexual deviations. The reader will recognize many of the classical deviations in "shadow" form as we discuss the practices of the "swingers," however.

Most of the sexual practices previously discussed have been known throughout man's history. Group sex as we shall describe it differs in that it is a relatively new aspect of behavior, a product of a pseudosophisticated and affluent society. It is so modern that the famed Kinsey report of 1948 indicated its lack of significance by dismissing it in one sentence. It is not considered at all in the classical studies of sex by Havelock Ellis. Forms of group sex are as old as mankind, but they did not have the aura of gentility nor the rationalizations and social connotations that we will encounter in this phenomenon.

There are no accurate figures on the number of couples presently involved in group sex, but there are organizations in most of the major cities, and an estimate of one-half to one million people appears conservative. The participants are mainly married, middle class suburbanites, very conservative in dress and politics, and generally people who do not belong to a cohesive social group or profession. There are no in-depth clinical studies of them, but this may indicate either that they do not come to medical attention very often or that the phenomenon is too new. Most writings about group sex are either descriptive or sociological in nature or are based upon a few cases that have come to psychiatric attention.

The origin of the swinging movement is obscure. Its close relative, wife-lending or some form of wife exchange, has been a part of the cultural patterns of many so-called "primitive" societies. The practice of wife-lending usually was of a definite service to the specific tribe or organization that practiced it, and it was an accepted part of everyday life rather than being a social oddity. A common factor to the societies that practiced wife-lending was that sex was looked upon as a normal and fairly unemotional animal phenomenon much as any other physiological function necessary for life and the preservation of the species. The sharing of one's wife was a sign of trust and friendship with no thought of shame or wrongness entering the picture, and in some groups, it became a necessary part of social etiquette. The purely sexual aspect was of minor significance, and sex, in general, had no connotations of sinfulness, evil, dirt, or any other negative aspect attached to it.

The American culture is over-sexualized. (Over-sexualized is not synonymous with over-sexed!) This sexualization is carried to the extreme in everything from selling automobiles to promoting behavioral norms. The unspoken message is that a full sex life is assurance of near-utopian happiness and that success in life is measured by the number and quality of one's sexual escapades. The stereotyped male image is the young, attractive, sexual athlete who selects his nightly mate from a bevy of beauties all fighting to sleep with him. The young female controls men by the flick of a false eyelash glued to a painted lid and may use her body to produce everything from religious adulation to jealous murder. Reality is reality, however, and only fantasies of these stereotypes actually are available for the vast majority of middle class Americans.

Group sex, or swinging, is one method of acting out these all-American fantasies. The ugly words "infidelity" and "adultery" are replaced by the innocuous term "swinging." That which was evil and anti-social becomes good, pleasant, and evidence of sophisticated advancement. This show of "left bank" liberality appears to be of extreme importance to the swingers who otherwise tend to lead relatively dull and colorless, even ultra-conservative, lives. They are able to reinforce each other's fantasies of hypersexuality in a manner resembling that seen in adolescent gangs.

The other segment of the great American fantasy is its obsession with youth, and one also sees this in the swinging groups. Enormous efforts are made to retain the illusion of youth physically, and perhaps the main motivation behind the sexual preoccupation is the attempt to foster this illusion. Most of the participants are in or are approaching middle age.

Swinging differs basically from the true sexual deviations in that it does not appear to be either compulsive or impulsive in nature. It is a conscious and premediated activity which requires not only controlled planning but also planning in concert with others. The first step in this process is the making of a contact. This can occur through word of mouth from friends or acquaintances who perceive that there is some mutual sexual attraction that can be capitalized upon, or occasionally the initiation occurs through chance contacts at a club or bar. However, most contacts probably occur through one of a variety of published media. This infers, of course, that the individual was reading that publication for a reason and that the contact was not forced upon him; at some level of consciousness he was looking for it.

There are many of these titilating publications available to swingers. They have such names as *Kindred Spirits, Swinger's Life, Swinging, Select,* and *Liberality*. Descriptive ads may be placed for a fee, and revealing photographs of the advertiser in suggestive poses may or may not be included, for a bit extra, of course. The publication usually uses a box number for those answering an advertisement that may be identified only by a code word or number. Some require those answering the ad to enclose a small fee as a partial defense against the idle curious and as a way of increasing the profits.

One such publication, now defunct, out of Trenton, New Jersey, stated in a 1969 ad, "Sophisticated couple with large Manhattan apartment would like to meet liberal-minded, attractive couple interested in all varieties of culture." The "all varieties of culture" means all varieties of sexual activities. For example, had they wished to specify primarily oral sex, they would have said, "French culture."

Another advertisement stated, "He, 6 ft., 190 lbs. of cultured satisfaction. She, 5 ft. 3 in., 120 lbs, of lucious blonde. Both looking for refined young marrieds (25 to 30) who want new and better ways to enjoy living. Willing to experiment." The last sentence signifies their willingness to engage in, or at least to discuss the possibility of engaging in variations of sexual activities. The words, "refined," "intelligent," "sophisticated," and "cultured" appear so frequently in the advertisements that the reader must wonder if there is not too much protesting!

Most of these publications are very careful to word the ads and to disguise the pictures so as to avoid identification of the clients and to forestall difficulty with the postal authorities. Others that do not use the mails and are more uncensored are sold in the "adult only" book stalls in most of the larger cities. Many examples will be found in the bookstores in the vicinity of 42nd Street and Broadway in New York City.

These publications do not restrict themselves solely to advertisements for swingers. Many of the more obviously deviant sexual practices are alluded to or described so that little is left to the imagination of the reader. It is characteristic of subcultures that they concoct a system of nouns and adjectives that they feel are unique to themselves. A secret code or an exclusive language gives a sense of superiority and cohesiveness which otherwise is nonexistent. (Parents of teen-agers will be very familiar with this phenomenon!) Most of these terms are designed to make the deviant acts sound more acceptable and less pathological and perhaps even to be unintelligible to the uninitiated. For example, sado-masochistic practices are referred to as "discipline," and the practice of restraining an individual with ropes or chains to a bed or chair is referred to as "bondage." "Greek culture" refers to anal intercourse, and "Roman culture" is used to indicate a true orgy. Other symbols and phrases are used to indicate homosexuality, bisexuality, and fetishism, but the scientific terms are rarely used.

The actual swinging, or group sex, may occur in many contexts. There are swinging clubs and societies that have regularly planned parties and picnics that may include renting a large portion of a club, hotel, or motel. Most swinging probably occurs in private homes in suburbia with only two or three couples involved at any one time, but grouping together in large parties now and then may help the participants reassure themselves that their acts constitute an accepted way of life and that they are not aberrant in behavior. Large groups also make for more partners to choose from and make it easier to avoid teaming up with the same couple several times.

If the couples have not swung together previously, they are likely to meet at a private home, and there is apt to be a rather ritualized prelude to the first sexual contacts. Much of the prelude is designed to get acquainted and to allow a couple to change its mind without injuring the feelings of either of the concerned parties. Some verbal sparring of no consequence may grow into sexualized conversation which eventually may lead to the showing of pornographic pictures or movies. All of this is likely to be facilitated with relaxing amounts of alcohol. Drinking, perhaps to overcome the ingrained inhibitions, appears to be an essential part of the swinging society, but that is equally true of most modern gatherings for pure pleasure.

If the initial contact is a disappointment to one of the couples and it wishes to withdraw, this can be done by claiming that the wife has just started a menstrual period, or that she has had a recent abortion and has begun to have some difficulty. This allows a graceful retreat from an unpleasant situation.

The sexual behavior is also quite ritualized. An evening of "closed swinging" means that the couples exchange partners and go their separate ways for some specified amount of time in private. They then rejoin, and if they are spending the night at the host's home, husbands and wives are apt to end up sleeping together. "Open swinging" refers to sexual acts carried on either in the same beds or same rooms or in some open manner so that other people have easy access to the action at any time. This type of swinging almost resembles an ongoing card game in which visitors may kibitz at will! In its extreme form it approaches "Roman culture"—an orgy.

The sexual activity, open or closed, rarely is restricted to simple intercourse. The oral activities, cunnilingus and fellatio, are included in most swinging sessions, but fellatio performed on the male by the female rarely continues to orgasm. This is not so true of cunnilingus. Many male swingers feel that this is a far more certain and satisfactory method of leading the female partner to orgasm than is straight intercourse, and most female participants agree. In open swinging, several of these acts may be occurring simultaneously between three or more people. For example, while a woman performs fellatio on a man lying on a bed, another man has intercourse with her dog fashion.

Homosexual activities among male swingers appears to be a strict no-no. This certainly is true of open swinging at the larger gatherings, although there is some question about its actual rarity when one peruses the advertisements in swinging publications. This attitude about male homosexuality is in marked contrast to the frequency with which women engage in sexual activities with each other at swinging parties; in fact, one study stated that homosexual acts occurred with over 90 percent of the women observed at one large gathering of swingers. The female activity usually begins with breast and body fondling, but the preferred ending is mutual cunnilingus.

The women do not have complete freedom for their homosexual activities, however. Even here there appears to be a ritualization and certain unwritten rules. Most commonly the pairing off of females does not occur until after they have had intercourse with one or more of the males. The girls may then get together at random, but it is tacitly forbidden that they do this alone. The men like to get their "second wind" while observing the homosexual activities of the females, and some of them have stated a particular pleasure in watching their wives so engaged. The men may simply observe, but more frequently they make kibitzing comments not unlike that of observers at any other sports event! Masturbation while observing others is permissible.

Swingers use many methods to heighten their sexual enjoyment and to whet flagging sexual appetites. The use of pornographic pictures and movies has been mentioned, but another common method is some form of a mechanical vibrator. These gadgets are on display in many shops and drug stores in almost every city. One which sells for $5.98 in many suburban drug stores is advertised as a "neck massager," but the vibrating segment of the machine has such an undeniable penis configuration and size that not even the most innocent observer could mistake its actual intended use. (A Miami shop in a large resort hotel had several in different sizes and colors.) Although the male may use the vibrator on scrotum or perineal region, it most frequently is used by the female. Rarely is it a substitute for intercourse, but rather it is used as a prelude to or in association with it. It is considered good manners for the host couple of a swinging party to have at least one vibrator available for the guests to use.

Words also are used as aids to sexual stimulation. Bona fide anatomical and physiological terms such as penis, vagina, and intercourse rarely are heard. This is equally true of the terminology for the many variations of intercourse and other sexual acts. Street terms, frequently to the point of gross obscenity, are used so frequently and in such a manner that one must conclude that they have their own psychological value, above and beyond communication, to the swingers. This, as mentioned in a previous chapter, is a practice not confined to swingers, and it is one with a definite dynamic meaning; that is, it gives an aura of badness, evil, and forbiddenness to sex and removes it from the realms of tenderness and love—taboo areas in swinging groups.

Several other aspects of the swinging society give interesting insights into the psyche of its participants. One of these is the almost fanatical care taken to avoid a close relationship, as alluded to above. So great an effort is made to avoid full personal identification that last names rarely are given. A man usually divulges only broad generalities about his job or profession, and all of the conversation remains on a nonpersonal and superficial level. This may indicate a basic distrust among swingers, but combined with other observable characteristics, it certainly shows a great reluctance to foster closeness and intimacy; and yet, this desire for closeness and intimacy is given as one of the main reasons for entering the swinging society!

Another sign of the desire to avoid a lasting relationship is the infrequency with which swinging couples make second or third engagements with each other. Swingers rationalize this by saying that they wish to seek a wide variety of interesting and exciting people rather than to confine themselves to a narrow group, but if this is the whole answer, it seems to indicate a never-ending search. Perhaps there are exceptions to this, but almost all observers of swinging groups have remarked upon this phenomenon of one-time-only meetings. Obviously this does not refer to that variety of swinging in which two couples regularly exchange mates. This is not properly called group sex or swinging since it is confined to mate swapping only, and since it does not conform to the ritualizations discussed.

The liberality of swingers does not stretch to include single people; especially not single males. It is assumed that a single person is much more apt to cause trouble in the form of jealousies, but the single girl is not considered so great a risk. This may be due to the fact that men take the lead in swinging society, and that they are not anxious to encourage competition. It is very rare to find a swinging couple in which the female has taken the initiative.

Let us take a closer look at some of the individual psychodynamics of this interesting sexual phenomenon. The voyeuristic element on the part of the male is very obvious at the swinging parties. It has been observed that no man, no matter how jaded from previous sexual encounters, is ever too tired to watch someone else having sexual activities. This, for many men, seems to be the most enjoyable part of swinging. Of course, the man is more limited than the woman in filling a whole evening with sexual activities unless he avoids ejaculation. Unlike his female counterpart, the man who can rest a few minutes then go again and again to orgasm is a rarity. Especially popular among the men is a chance to observe two females performing cunnilingus upon each other, as previously mentioned.

The opposite pole of voyeurism is exhibitionism. This does not appear to be an element in all swingers, for some simply will not or cannot perform openly. There is some reason to believe, however, that the male who can maintain an erection and perform sexual intercourse before an audience has strong exhibitionistic tendencies. Although exhibitionism, strictly speaking, is a male device, the frequency with which female swingers will perform homosexually before a male audience (estimated at over 90 percent) appears to need no interpretation! Both male and female swingers place great emphasis on body configuration and breast and penis size. Breasts enlarged by plastic implants are very popular among female swingers, despite the fact that the men find them too firm and inanimate. Much of the participants' gratification appears to come from the impression they make upon the observing associates by a display of anatomy.

The latent homosexual element of the male swinger requires attention. It was mentioned that male homosexual activities virtually are forbidden in the swinging culture, while female homosexual activities are not only allowed, but are encouraged by males and females alike. This phenomenon would indicate the possibility of a great need for the male to guard himself against any possible homosexual temptations because of his unconscious desires for them. Homosexuality is diametrically opposed to the hypermasculine image the male swinger wishes to project of himself.

The psychoanalysts have spoken of the homosexual element in the male who encourages his wife to have intercourse with another man, and especially of the male who desires to watch this. One explanation is that the latent homosexuality in the husband is vicariously gratified through an unconscious identification with his wife who has had or is having intercourse with another man.

The relationship of this factor to the madonna-prostitute syndrome previously discussed appears obvious. The man not only knows that his wife is having intercourse with other men (prostituting herself), but he knows that she probably is practicing many unusual forms of sexual activity with him. Many of these practices are considered degrading or at least abnormal in middle class society, the social segment to which swingers usually belong. Does this fill a need in the male—a need to debase his wife in order that he may then be more potent with her? An integral part of the swinging culture is that a couple discuss these sexual activities in detail with each other at the conclusion of the party or the swinging session.

One wife who entered swinging with extreme reluctance drew the line at "open" swinging despite constant encouragement from her husband. Each time she "swung" with another man, her husband put her through what she called "twenty questions." He quizzed her about every aspect of her relationship with her partner, and would not be satisfied with less than a minute by minute account. The woman told this after she had changed her mind about the whole thing and was seeking advice about a divorce.

These "postmortem" discussions between husband and wife point to another interesting element in the psychodynamics of swinging. The discussions usually are carefully worded so as to avoid any possible injury to the ego of the spouse. The negative aspect of the evening's partner or partners will be accented, and every effort will be made to avoid an indication that the evening's temporary partner was sexually better than or more able to satisfy than the spouse. A frequent qualifying phrase in any description of the evening's mate will be, "But not as good as you."

This necessity for constant ego support, especially for the male, is further evidenced by the almost fanatical need for the male to satisfy the female. This is a matter of great pride, and if for some reason or other the woman does not have an orgasm, her swinging partner takes it as a personal attack on his sexual abilities. For one thing he knows that she is apt to spread the word about that he was not good at "Frenching" or at whatever activity he practiced. There is much talk among the men about how many times one can have an orgasm in an evening, and many of the stories about this have all the credibility of a Mark Twain tall tale. The men are extremely flattered by the female who compliments their sexual activities, and this too is an accepted part of the swinging culture's code of courtesy.

We began by questioning whether or not swinging should be included in a book on the sexual deviations. We have not entirely answered the question, and the reader must draw his own conclusion. That there are elements of many of the sexual deviations in the swingers appears certain, but we have emphasized throughout that all of the true deviations also have their representations in the psychosexual levels of the normal personality. The few professionals who have studied the swinging groups and societies closely have concluded, by and large, that the participants are no more nor less "sick" than the average middle class North American suburbanite. This, however, may not be entirely complimentary!

The reader will note that group sex as here discussed did not refer to communal sex nor to promiscuity. The difference is marked. The practitioners of group sex go to great extremes to avoid detection and to preserve the superficial amenities of middle class suburbia in everyday living. They are rebelling only on the sexual level, and far from attempting to promote true communal living, they are competitive and egocentric even in sex. They seek particularly to embellish life with experiences that will give it meaning beyond the day-to-day grind, and yet they appear to lack the resources to look beyond the most basic level—the sexual. Unlike the members of the communes, they seek not to establish a new order or even to upset the old; they hunt only for personal pleasure. Also unlike the devotees of the communes, swingers tend to protect their children from knowledge of their activities and to raise them within the establishment. Many state that it makes them uncomfortable for another person's child to catch them in bed with its mother or father. One can imagine that the desire to keep the activity a secret from children stems from guilt, or that it merely indicates a discretion normal to most parents and their sexual lives.

The swingers accent that their marital relations are improved by their activities. They insist that the sexual freedom of swinging increases their appreciation of their respective spouses. Just how or why this would be true is somewhat elusive and perhaps even contradictory, since one reason for swinging is presumably to have new and unusual experiences not available at home.

There is little reason to believe that their search for pleasure poses a threat to society or that it impinges upon the rights or safety of others. Perhaps it is most logical to view the activities of the participants in group sex simply as interesting variations of human behavior that should be of little concern to the nonparticipants. The growth of the practice may be one other indication of the lack of belonging to a cohesive group that appears so widespread in our society. More and more people appear isolated from meaningful, lasting relationships, and so they turn to more and more unusual means of making themselves feel a part of this world and of producing some pleasure in life. Group sex may be one of these means. To each his own!

15

Miscellaneous Deviations

THIS CHAPTER WILL include a variety of deviant sexual practices that may be diagnostic entities, but that are more likely to be components or symptoms of some other personality disorders. Most of them are either statistically so rare as to be relatively insignificant from both the medical and social viewpoint, or they are overshadowed by a related condition. They primarily are of interest to show the unlimited possibilities for the maldevelopment of human sexuality. It literally would be impossible to delineate every single method by which the sexual drive may be expressed since there appears to be virtually no limit to the aberrations of the human mind in this sphere. The reader should recognize that many of these deviant acts represent variations upon, or components of, the more recognized clinical syndromes discussed in previous chapters.

UROPHILIA (UROLAGNIA)

Urophilia refers to the condition in which urine or the act of urination is strongly endowed with erotic significance. There may be both active (urinating upon) or passive (being urinated upon) forms. This condition represents a form of infantile sexuality that has persisted into adulthood. The child normally endows the act of urination with sexual significance, and many children believe that the father urinates into the mother's vagina during the sexual act. Some of these people do not lose this concept with time and physical maturation, and in these individuals urination may become a prerequisite to orgasm. Urolagnia may exist in both male and female and may be a part of heterosexuality or homosexuality. As with most of the sexual deviations, innumerable variations and modifications occur.

Mr. Jefferson was a successful, middle-aged civic leader in a large midwestern city. He was married and the father of three children. He was what he appeared to be 99 percent of the time—a very conservative, middle class businessman noted for his gentleness and mild manner. However, every four to six months, Mr. Jefferson felt impelled to deviate from his usual manner of living. He would travel to a neighboring city on the pretext of business and make contact with a call girl at the hotel where he habitually stayed. He would engage the girl for the evening, wine and dine her luxuriantly in his hotel suite, pay handsomely for her time and ask only one thing in return. She would be asked to abstain from urination during the evening for as long as possible. When it became a matter of urination or else for her, Mr. Jefferson would quickly undress and lie on his back on the floor while the girl, who had simultaneously stripped, squatted above him and urinated into his mouth. Sometimes he followed this act with intercourse with the girl, but more often than not he masturbated to orgasm, and that terminated the evening. Mr. Jefferson could then return to his rather staid routine of normalcy for another period of months.

Some urophiliacs prefer to urinate upon the female as a prelude to intercourse with her, but it can act as a substitute for intercourse. Homosexual men may spray each other with urine before engaging in other forms of sexual activity. A few women have reported that intercourse to orgasm was possible only when the man first urinated into the vagina. This appears to be the only significant form of urophilia in females. There are few, if any, female counterparts of Mr. Jefferson.

The psychological significance of urophilia resembles that of other practices in which the sexual act must be endowed with the disgust and the filth ordinarily associated with excretory functions. It also may have a hostile component since the act of urinating upon someone is generally considered the height of insult in our society. Mr. Jefferson, in allowing himself to be urinated upon by the female, was expressing his need to subjugate himself to the all-powerful woman, and simultaneously, he was showing his contempt for males.

Coprophilia

Coprophilia and urophilia are closely related and differ only in degree. The sexual significance of defecation to the child has been a matter of much psychiatric discussion since the days of Sigmund Freud. Coprophilia, like urophilia, represents a rather extreme infantile sexualism carried into adulthood. Perhaps even more than urophilia, coprophilia indicates a need to endow the sexual act with extreme disgust; perhaps the most extreme disgust possible. The specific acts of coprophilia may include variations upon either watching defecation or having contact with the feces. It differs from urophilia in that it almost always is confined to the male. In actual practice, the male usually seeks his coprophiliac activities with paid prostitutes simply because it is difficult to persuade "normal" female partners to cooperate.

French houses of prostitution once recognized and catered to the coprophiliac impulses of their customers by installing glass bottomed "bidets" which allowed for the observation of excreting acts. Apparently the practice never became popular in the United States, but then we have spread a puritanical curtain over even the normal pleasures, let alone those of questionable standing such as coprophilia.

We are a very bowel conscious people who spend millions of dollars annually upon laxatives to control a body function which would regulate itself 99 percent of the time if allowed to do so. Few physicians will deny that they have many patients who are obsessed with bowel movements, yet who appear to be unaware of the pleasure they derive from defecation. That the act is a source of pleasure to a child must be obvious to all who have reared children. The infant must be taught to disassociate sexual pleasure from defecation and to endow the act with the disgust and shame that pleases the adult world. He frequently gives up his freedom to enjoy his defecation and its products with great reluctance. Many things can go awry in this maturing process since it is so highly charged with emotion.

One coprophiliac was a forty-two-year-old practicing physician highly valued in his community. He had been quite successful in persuading several of his female patients to allow him to observe them in the act of defecation. He had persuaded them by spurious but convincing arguments that it would greatly aid him in his diagnostic procedures. He did not otherwise touch them nor make sexual advances of any kind toward them. This practice came to light when he entered psychotherapy for a related personality disorder, but the coprophilia part of his existence was otherwise insignificant.

This physician demonstrated how the retention of one infantile segment of the personality frequently is associated with others. He also wished to nurse lactating females as if he were an infant. He had persuaded several of his postdelivery patients to allow him to taste their breast milk as a method of "testing" it for the babies. One patient with whom he had a very intimate but otherwise nonsexual relationship had allowed him to lie in bed with her and nurse from both of her breasts twice daily for several weeks after her baby had been given up for adoption at birth.

This man was known as a busy and devoted physician in his rural community. He practiced his deviant acts in a nearby large city without detection for several years. Gradually be became more and more unstable and erratic in behavior until he first came into treatment for drug abuse in his late thirties. Coprophilia was only one of his many problems.

Pornography

Pornography in this sense refers to a condition in which pornographic literature, usually pictures, becomes an end in itself rather than a stimulation for or a normal prelude to sexual intercourse. That pornographic literature is extremely popular and that all who find interest in it are not sexual deviates goes without further discussion. It, too, is primarily a male activity since the female finds far less sexual stimulation from viewing erotic scenes or reading erotic literature.

The most common use of pornography is by an individual, usually a very inadequate feeling male, who views his collection of pictures or pamphlets as an aid to masturbation. Unless this is the exclusive sexual outlet, one is hard-pressed to call this a sexual deviation, and it is without doubt considered normal in adolescence.

Mr. Jones came to psychiatric consultation at the insistence of his wife to whom he had been married for approximately twenty years. She stated that she had been aware of his habits of collecting pictures of nude women in suggestive poses since shortly after marriage. He had cloaked this as long as possible under the guise of an "art collection," but she had begun to disbelieve this after he had become relatively impotent before age forty. She did not have insight into the situation, and she actually felt that he was avoiding her because he was having an affair with some other woman.

This was not so; in fact, Mr. Jones had never had intercourse or any other sexual contact with any woman except his wife. He did have an extensive collection of nude females and some pictures of men and women in heterosexual activities, and in his imagination he had copulated with hundreds of lovely women, but only in fantasy. He masturbated an average of twice a day while looking at these pictures, but otherwise he carried on his life as a rural postman without any indication of his private habit. The development of impotence was merely symptomatic of the feelings of sexual inadequacy with which he had struggled all his life. It is not infrequent that such feelings intensify with approaching middle age and become manifested by some degree of impotency.

The psychological significance of the substitution of pornographic literature for a more overt heterosexual life is twofold. First, the man is apt to feel, as so many of our subjects, that he is inadequate to relate heterosexually to living females. Second, he fears and is made uncomfortable by close interpersonal contacts with females, and he prefers to use his fantasy because it simply represents distance and safety to him.

A discussion of pornography must include something about its relationship to sexual crimes. Some feel that pornographic literature incites youngsters to abnormal sexuality and that it encourages criminal and immoral activities. The truth is that we have no evidence to support this idea. Nothing we know of the genesis of the sexual deviations or of the causes of excessive or criminal sexual behavior indicates that pornography plays a causative role. The president's commission appointed to study the question published an extensive report of several hundred pages in September, 1970. This commission was composed of some of the nation's leading experts in the field of human sexual behavior. They concluded that no connection between crime, immorality, and pornography existed. This conclusion agreed with the anecdotal experiences of most authorities on human sexual behavior. Unfortunately, the findings of this learned commission were ignored completely by the White House.

The etiology of sexual deviation lies in the preschool years primarily. Certainly the seeds of the conditions are sown long before the child learns to read sufficiently to understand pornography. Secondly, most sexual offenders do not read pornographic literature—they do not read literature of any kind. The largest amount of pornography is bought and read by middle aged men whose lives are quiet tributes to passivity, men who would be the last to commit a crime of any type. Those who champion censorship of pornographic literature may do so on esthetic grounds, but they cannot logically do so on the basis of crime prevention.

Coprolalia

Coprolalia refers to the practice of deriving sexual stimulation from the use of obscene language during lovemaking, or rarely, sexual gratification from the use of the language alone. Variations include the practice of writing obscenities upon walls, usually in public bathrooms, and receiving gratification from the knowledge that the message will be read by others. This type of individual usually assumes that the person who reads the obscene graffiti will be stimulated by it. Via this vicarious route, he established a long distance sexual contact with another person. Since the obscenities usually are written in public rooms frequented only by men, the homosexual element is suggested in that one man sexually stimulates another.

Coprolalia in a minor form is so common as to be virtually normal. It is considered a deviation only when it becomes an absolute requirement to erotic arousal or when it becomes an end in itself.

One woman, forty years of age and the mother of two

daughters, stated that she had never been able to achieve orgasm during twenty years of marriage to two husbands without the stimulation of what she termed "gutter talk." She would request that her sexual partner speak in graphic terms of what he was doing to her and what he would like to do to her, and that he describe these fantasied acts in the worst possible language. This knowledge came to light as part of a routine history, but it played little if any significance in the woman's life style. She did not consider it abnormal, and it was in no way anxiety provoking to her. It only bothered her in that her second husband felt that it was nonsense and sometimes would not play the game. She had absolutely no sexual arousal, not even vaginal lubrication, when he would not cooperate.

One male, Mr. Johnson, requested virtually the same sort of conversation from his wife. He was able to maintain an erection and to complete intercourse without the coprolalia; but he found sex a much more pleasant and gratifying procedure when this language was used. He would ask his wife to fantasize that he had a penis the size of an elephant's and to draw him detailed word pictures of how it felt and of what it was doing to her. His wife objected to the practice during the first year of marriage because it conflicted with her staunch fundamentalistic religious background. She gradually overcame her scruples so that she also began to find it a helpful accompaniment to lovemaking.

The psychological significance of coprolalia should now be perfectly obvious to the reader who has proceeded this far. The dual meanings, seen in many of the sexual practices discussed, are: degradation of the woman and the sexual act and exaltation of the man's somewhat doubted manhood.

Pygmalionism

Pygmalionism refers to a condition in which there is an unrealistic love for an idealized object rather than for an actual person. In a finer sense, it also refers to a need for the male to produce his own loved object. It usually exists in rather covert forms in which the loved object is placed on a pedestal while the actual relationship remains platonic. The relationship of pygmalionism to the madonna-prostitute complex is that these men so deify their loved objects that they frequently find themselves unable to treat them in an overtly sexual manner. They become untouchable.

Some men may "adopt" streetwalkers or women far beneath their social scale and attempt to make them over into the idealized object of their fantasies. They may, in fact, be successful, but then they find that they have created an object to which they cannot successfully relate in a heterosexual manner. Whether or not this should be classified as a sexual deviation is a moot question. Certainly it is an abnormality only in the extreme and not in the milder forms, and even when it stems from pathology, it may appear as an act of kindness to the casual observer. Perhaps there is a small amount of pygmalionism in many who are concerned about the welfare of others and who do something about it.

Mixoscopia

Mixoscopia refers to the deviation in which sexual excitement and gratification are derived from watching others in the sexual act. Although it is a variation on both the madonna-prostitute syndrome and voyeurism, it is a more generic term including gratification from all forms of passive looking. It occurs in a variety of situations, both with married couples and among single males. It is relatively rare among females; in fact, there is question about whether or not it exists with them in pure form.

Tom was a policeman of approximately four years' experience with the force. He was considered an excellent officer and was in line for the officer's training program.

No one had the faintest idea that Tom's hobby was frequenting the byways known to be favorite parking spots for lovers, finding a pair having intercourse, or at least working up to it, and forcing them to continue while he spotted them with a flashlight. Tom came to psychiatric consultation when he inadvertently chose the wrong victims one night. The couple he occosted at an isolated spot engaging in intercourse on a blanket happened to be his sergeant and a girl friend! That was the end of Tom's promising career in the police department!

The following vignette is used to illustrate mixoscopia, but it could represent the madonna-prostitute syndrome equally well. Mrs. Berger forced her husband into the clinic after he had made her have intercourse with a perfect stranger while he watched and masturbated. He appeared unable to comprehend why she was so upset about this relatively harmless desire of his, and after a brief consultation, she forgave him, and they did not return. This sort of a reaction of forgiveness, by no means rare, leads one to question the role of the female in the interaction. Has she, by some means, encouraged her husband in his habit?

Mixoscopia differs from voyeurism in that the true voyeur must have his observations surreptitious and forbidden if he is to be gratified. It also differs in that a mixoscopic male may use his own wife as an object, whereas as this is extremely uncommon in voyeurism.

Nymphomania and Satyriasis

Nymphomania and satyriasis refer to sexual insatiability, female and male forms respectively. Popular sexual mythology would have these conditions represent some high plane of sexual pleasure, but nothing is further from the truth. These people are driven by forces beyond their control to seek a sexual gratification which never can be found, and the search becomes a compulsion devoid of the usual components of emotion and purely mechanical in nature. The conditions always represent underlying emotional problems which go far beyond the purely sexual.

Mary S was brought to the psychiatric clinic by her parents. She had been a behavioral problem since early childhood, but not until she became sexually mature had she become uncontrollable. The episodes leading to the consultation were typical. Her parents had discovered that in three evenings she had completed intercourse with members of two fraternity houses, over seventy boys, on the campus where she was a freshman. She estimated that she had had intercourse with over five hundred boys by her eighteenth year, and even if one discounts her figure, it remains phenomenal. She literally refused no male who asked her, and she was not backward in letting her intentions be known.

Mary's sexual episodes came in spurts. She sometimes went weeks with all the behavior of a puritanical deaconness, only to revert to her compulsive sexual activity despite good resolutions during her reformed period. During her periods of good behavior she considered all sex as sinful and forbidden. Even during the periods of peak sexual activity, she did not actually enjoy the sex act. She had never had an orgasm, although she always acted the part. Sexual intercourse was her way of seeking relationships and popularity. She became the center of attraction and fantazied herself as a person of fame and importance, but the other side of the coin was that she also saw herself as the scum of the earth. Psychiatric examination revealed that Mary was a deeply disturbed girl, a borderline psychotic.

Satyriasis, the male form, indicates great sexual immaturity, or even profound instability. Sometimes it is the symptom of a psychotic condition such as schizophrenia or manic depression, hypomanic phase. For example, one man's wife insisted upon his hospitalization after he had begun demanding intercourse ten to twenty times daily. Upon examination he was found to be under the impression that

God had commanded him to do many things, including the frequent sexual acts. He, like Mary S, while presenting with a sexual disorder, suffered from a more pervasive condition.

SALIROMANIA

This very peculiar and uncommon sexual deviation refers to sexual excitement and gratification achieved by deliberately soiling or damaging women's clothing, statues, or the paintings of nude females. The behavior appears to be compulsive and impulsive and to have a heavy sadistic tinge to it. It is derived from a strong impulse to degrade and show contempt for the female sex. The infliction of actual damage or harm to living human beings, if it occurs at all, is purely accidental. Its aggressive and hostile components are rather obvious, but they are expressed by symbolization and displacement. Thus the clothing or the representation of the female is used to symbolize the atcual person, and the anger and hatred are displaced upon this symbol.

In one sense, it is a far safer way of expressing anger than taking it out upon the human being. It may precede sexual intercourse, but it can also substitute for it. In the latter instance, the act of tearing up the garment, the most common form, may be followed by masturbation and ejaculation upon the garment; an expression of both aggression and contempt. In this act one recognizes the relationship to fetishism as well as sadism. The condition usually occurs in young men who are withdrawn, aloof—true "loners" who find all interpersonal relationships uncomfortable and threatening. Many will be found to be schizophrenic upon closer examination.

NECROPHILIA

Sexual attraction to dead bodies is a rare condition with horrifying overtones often expressed in the world's literature on vampirism, grave robbing, and other ghoulish activities thought by some to be totally fictional. This is not so, and the human imagination cannot exceed the acts that have been recorded.

The necrophile, perhaps more frequently than any other single deviant, borders upon the psychotic. His hold upon reality is tenuous, or in many instances, has already broken. Those who have advanced to the horrifying, but fortunately very rare, state of necrophogia (eating the dead), obviously are not totally sane, but the other end of the spectrum, merely becoming sexually aroused by helpless (dead) objects, is a different story.

The necrophile represents the highest degree of sexual inferiority. He sees himself totally inept, not only sexually, but as a man. He cannot conceive of a live female who would be so degraded as to submit to his advances. Death represents the acme of helplessness and allows him to fantasize that he possesses power and vigor. A variation of this need, and one showing far less pathology than true necrophilia, is seen in men who request their sexual partners to lie perfectly immobile, therefore, to act "as if" they were dead. Such men may lose all sexual interest if the woman moves.

There is another side to this psychopathology. By now the reader knows that mental and emotional states never exist in simple, clearcut cause and effect relationships, but like diamonds, have multiple facets. The necrophile is no exception. His bizarre behavior also represents an attempt to make the sexual act so repulsive and disgusting as to destroy the desire for it. His hope is not realized, and he is forced to repeat it.

The necrophile of fiction obtains his victims by magical means or by grave robbing. The latter method is still reported, but many times authorities assume that a robbed grave represents an attempt to steal jewelry and adornments. The necrophiliac aspect of grave robbing may be far more important that we actually know. Most frequently, however, the necrophile obtains access to the dead in morgues and funeral homes where he seeks employment. He may pass unnoticed in the community and live a secluded, lonely life, because his victims cannot report him!

KT was an embalmer by trade. He was single, a quiet, unassuming man in his early thirties. He had no apparent family or friends. He had worked in many funeral homes throughout the south but rarely over six to nine months in any one town. He had been a valued worker in each of his jobs since he knew his job and he appeared unconcerned about length of hours, working conditions, or even income. Most often he was satisfied with a small room in the funeral parlor and very meager pay.

KT had been fired from his job only two times. Upon the first occasion he had incited the rage of the owner of the establishment when he had been discovered fondling the breasts of a young girl who had just been brought in. He denied ever having done such a thing before, but he left without objection.

His next and final apprehension came almost two years later when he was working in a small town in the southeast. He was discovered having intercourse with a female corpse which he was preparing to embalm. He was severely beaten by the other employees—so severely that hospitalization was necessary. It was during this hospitalization that the above story was obtained.

This young man became a patient in a state mental hospital after recovery from his injuries, and his eventual outcome is unknown.

The necrophile who kills to obtain his bodies lies between the sadist and the true necrophile. He represents a combination of these morbid obsessions; a combination which creates a monster abhorrent to all. He has not been able to repress or to control his aggressive impulses so that his underlying rage at females occasionally breaks into the open in compelling force. Fortunately, he is very rare.

Gerontophilia

Gerontophilia refers to an exclusive and compulsive desire for sexual gratification with elderly mates of either sex. It does not include those cases of May-December unions in which a genuine affection exists, or to those in which there is a conscious motive to inherit an estate or profit in some manner. There are those people, male and female, who do not get sexually aroused by anyone not in the elderly age range, and it is these people to whom the term refers.

The dynamics of gerontophilia are obscure since cases rarely come to treatment, and the condition is not a legal offense. It appears that some people become gerontophiles through a fixation on grandparental figures, but that others feel too inadequate to relate at their own age level. They feel that the elderly partner will be too grateful for the attention to notice the inadequacy. Perhaps even more of them represent extremes of unresolved Oedipal situations so that they continue to look for the parent as a lover.

An occasional gerontophile is also a rapist and the news media reports frequently point up the elderly victims. This type of rape incites horror and disgust more than usual, since society does not connect sexuality with aging. We prefer to think that parents and parent figures are asexual, and while rape always is abhorred, it is doubly so when the victim is elderly.

Polymorphous Perversion

The term refers to the uncommon man whose behavior demonstrates infantalism in numerous sexual areas. He may combine homosexuality with pedophilia, sadism, voyeurism, and urophilia, for example. He shows the signs and symptoms of a confusing array of sexual deviations, but does not restrict himself to any one of them.

Martin was remanded to therapy by the court after being

found guilty of molesting his own four-year-old son. Martin was a twenty-nine-year-old musician whose full scale IQ was far above average (138). He eventually told the group to which he was assigned of his practices of homosexuality, pedophilia, exhibitionism, voyeurism, sadism, and other sexual variations that defy description. Despite his intelligence, he could not hold jobs and be self-supporting because he simply could not force himself to live by any structure. His infantile irresponsibility covered all areas of living, yet he was so charming and boyish that he was forever being rescued by women with more compassion than common sense.

Martin was able to function heterosexually in that he was married and had a child. However, his wife, at the time of marriage, had been only fourteen years old! Once she became an adult of seventeen, he became disinterested in her, and at the time of his arrest, he was dating a thirteen-year-old girl.

The polymorphous individual, like Martin, responds poorly to presently known therapy. There is so little in his ego structure upon which to build that it appears to be a losing battle. Psychiatry has no certain answer for them; they simply have not come beyond the cradle emotionally. Treatment, to be successful, would have to be long, arduous and intense, and few of these men are willing to invest in it.

Pyromania

There are deviant fragments in many aberrant acts that cannot be called deviations in themselves. For example, there is frequently a large sexual component in one form of arson. One twenty-four-year-old man, who was in prison for a two-year sentence for having burned a large building in which he was a night watchman, asked to see a psychiatrist. He had developed considerable insight into his need to set the fire in order to prove his power, but he had been horrified with the fact that he got an erection and was compelled to masturbate while watching the fire. He was basically a very religious person who felt that almost any show of sexuality was sinful, and while the fire-setting itself did not greatly bother him, this sinful sexual component of it created great anxiety.

The sexual significance of fire can be seen in many of our everyday expressions. We speak of animals being "in heat." There are "red-hot mamas," "flames of desire," and more recently, "hot pants." Few things are more attractive to people than fire and sex, and both appeal to some basic emotion that combines both adoration and terror. The pyromaniac does not start his fire, then leave the scene. He is impelled to watch and frequently to help those fighting the fire. This need of the arsonist to be a part of the action aids the legal authorities in their work to apprehend the fire bugs.

Pyromania obviously is a form of arson that excludes malicious burning or fire-setting for profit. It includes only that form in which the sexual component, conscious or unconscious, is a dominant factor.

Kleptomania

Kleptomania is another condition not properly classified as a sexual deviation but in which there is frequently a strong sexual component. Kleptomania usually affects females who are compelled to steal objects that are of no real value to them. If these stolen articles are elongated, stealing them may express an unconscious desire for the possession of the male penis. At other times stealing may simply represent a substitution of the thrill of risking apprehension for the thrill of sexual behavior that is unconsciously forbidden to the individual. The stolen objects often symbolize the love the kleptomaniac has not received in sufficient amount.

The "sexual" thrill associated with kleptomania may be a minor part of this compulsive disorder, and it should not be misleading. The kleptomaniac is not a "sex fiend" in any sense of the word, nor is she apt to be sexually abnormal in any way. The other aspects of kleptomania are far more significant than the sexual.

Breaking and entering, another form of stealing, is one of the most common crimes in the United States. Many times it is totally devoid of any sexual significance, but in some cases there is an actual erection and occasionally even an orgasm when the burglar enters the forbidden house. These individuals usually enter through the window and probably would do so even if the door were wide open. There is a resemblance here to the rapist in that it is necessary to "enter the forbidden" by stealth or force.

The sexual deviations fascinate us. They do so because they apppear so aberrant to human behavior, but equally so because they spring from the normal depths of each of us. Perhaps no sexual deviations, not even the most revolting of them, would appear abnormal through the mind of a one-year-old child. The unbridled impulses of infancy, modified and molded and occasionally disguised by a veneer of sophistication, produce the sexual deviations of adulthood.

Epilogue

MANY READERS WILL have been shocked by the accounts of the devious routes sometimes taken by human psychosexual development. Many others will have been unable to accept much of what was said and will have discounted it as the product of a vivid and somewhat warped imagination. Both of these reactions are understandable since we do not like to think that humans, and therefore ourselves, are so vulnerable to those events of childhood over which there is so little control. Some find it disquieting to think of sexual behavior as being on a continuum so that the normal and the abnormal are difficult to establish with consistency. They prefer to think in concrete terms of good and bad, right and wrong, and to think that we indeed are masters of our fates. It makes them anxious and uncomfortable to admit that so much of sexual behavior is not under the control of that elusive thing called will power. The veneer of civilization and sophistication thinly covers that which we prefer to think of as base and degrading and restricted solely to lower animals and to the dregs of society. In some unfortunate souls, this thin veneer breaks easily under stress.

All of the case examples in this book are authentic. Names and places have been changed to preclude identification and embarrassment, but the basic facts are unaltered. Most of the examples were chosen because they were fairly representative, and they could and they do fit a multitude of patients familiar to the medical world. Some of them have become friends of the author during the process of treatment, and mutual respect frequently has been the outcome of a hostile beginning. It would be good to say that all patients made a complete recovery, but that would be false and misleading. Actually, in some, the outcome has been tragic.

The reader should have noted that no single case example with an adequate past history was the product of a healthy home environment by the general standards of our society. In each case one or both parents had failed to furnish the child with identification models compatible with normal heterosexual development. The smooth transition from one developmental stage to another, beginning with infancy and ending with adult sexuality, was either halted or forced to veer from the expected path. The body and the intellect may have developed normally or even to superiority, but the very basis of identification, the answer to "Who am I?" and "What am I?", lagged far behind. Love and aggression remained one amorphous emotion in many cases. There is much of the infant in all of us, but in every single case of sexual deviation, one can identify gross sexual elements that were perfectly normal at some stage of infancy but which unfortunately remained active long past the appropriate age.

The reader well may ask what can be normal about a desire to watch another person defecate or to receive pleasure from playing with urine? All observant mothers know that a child is fascinated by both the acts and the products of elimination, and that he must be taught, sometimes with painful difficulty, that adults find this process a necessary but somewhat distasteful process and that they prefer to get rid of the products because they smell bad. Not so obvious, but equally true, is the fact that children do not easily separate the sexual functions from those of elimination. The close proximity of the organs of these two functions may cause confusion to the developing child. Elimination feels good and pleases mother, and although playing with these areas also feels good, it highly displeases mother. What is a child to think? Most children have enough love and approval from the parents to allow them to give up this infantile confusion and to advance on into adulthood, but not all are so fortunate.

Very rarely are all of the facets of infantile sexuality carried over intact into adulthood unless there is also a severe, pervasive emotional disorder present. When this does occur, it is called polymorphous perversion, as was mentioned in the chapter on miscellaneous disorders, or it represents a true psychosis. Here, more than in any of the less complex deviations, we see that personality development cannot be separated from sexual development. The more infantile the sexual aspect of adulthood, the more immature is the total personality structure. When only one segment of sexuality remains infantile, as in the exhibitionist or the heterosexual pedophile, the individual may function well within the average limits in all other aspects of his life. However, it is improbable that he will function to the fullest of his potential as a heterosexual male because no matter how mild, there will be some defect in his total maturation. We in psychiatry deliberately use the word "psychosexual" without even a hyphen to indicate that the psychic and the sexual aspects of a person cannot be separated.

This means that the treatment of the deviations requires psychological treatment of the total person. It literally requires some method by which emotional growth can be encouraged so that the sexual drive and orientation reach, or at least near, the adult level. Unfortunately, there are no shortcuts to a growth process that should have occurred many years earlier. It means at the very minimum several months, but usually years of psychiatric treatment, depending upon the severity and the duration of the patient's condition and his motivation to change. For one condition, transsexualism, there is no effective treatment short of a surgical transformation.

We have alluded upon several occasions to a major difficulty in the treatment of sexual deviants. It is their great tendency to deny, and the reader must keep in mind that this is an unconscious process, that they are ill or in need of corrective action. They frequently do not have the overt anxieties and discomforts that one usually sees with the neuroses or other emotional problems. They either deny their illness and rationalize that their actions are perfectly normal, or as in the case of some of the more bizarre habits, they concoct spurious reasons why the acts are simply unique to themselves and should be of no concern to others.

The astute reader might have recognized that there is a certain similarity between the sexual deviants and those persons addicted to alcohol and drugs. Their behavior also is patterned, compulsive, and repetitive. In each case, their acts appear to be beyond their control, and they share the same ability to deny their illnesses and to rationalize their behavior. Even though their behavioral patterns are obviously self-destructive and are producing major problems for those around them, they tend to persist in a manner very difficult for the observer to comprehend. It is important to keep in mind that these individuals rarely respond to logic, persuasion, or punishment, and that they lack the personality maturity to look at their own behavior from the viewpoint of others and to learn from experience as readily as the average man. That part of them that remains infantile responds to society as an infant and puts its own impulses and desires before any consideration for the surrounding environment. They are people compelled to relieve their anxieties by a pathological method of sexual behavior.

The very aspect of the sexual deviant that makes him a candidate for psychiatric treatment also makes him an undesirable patient. Psychiatrists in the past have avoided them, and even though there is some change of attitude in recent years, there still is a tendency to do so for several reasons.

First, the sexual deviant, like his alcoholic and addict cousin, is a "bad" patient. He tends to be unreliable in appointments and equally unreliable in paying his bills, even if he has the means to do so. He most likely comes to treatment only to please someone else, or because he is in trouble with the law or with some significant figure in his life. His heart simply is not invested in the idea of treatment or personal change. He usually terminates with the psychiatrist as soon as the outside pressure is relieved from him. Even when he does come to treatment, he tends to "play games" with the therapist and to avoid anxiety-provoking situations such as coming face to face with his own feelings of inadequacy.

Second, psychiatrists, like everyone else, like to get results. Experience has shown that the traditional methods of psychiatric treatment have not been a good answer to the severe personality disorders. Response comes slowly and painfully, if it comes at all. This has led the psychiatrists to invest their time in patients who are more apt to respond positively in a shorter period.

There are several reasons for the slow response of the sexual deviant to treatment, but only two are of interest to us here. One is the deviant's habitual method of controlling his own feelings of anxiety. We mentioned that he did this partially by "playing games" in therapy, but even more than this, he does it by "acting out" between treatment sessions. For example, a voyeur is apt to be compelled to go window peeping after an anxiety-provoking session with his therapist. The pedophile, in like manner, may seek a child with whom to have a sexual contact. The deviant sexual act becomes a "tranquilizer" and this prevents the deviant personality from ever really coming to grips with reality, and it allows the cycle to keep repeating itself.

Another reason is the depth of the pathology and the time of its existence. It appears that the roots of the deviations are in early childhood and that the patient has come to accept the condition as a normal part of him. It does not "hurt," as it were, and people do not seek medical help unless they are hurting!

Psychiatry does not claim to have the final answer to the prevention or to the treatment of the sexual deviants, although group psychotherapy is believed by many to be the treatment of choice. Behavioral modification is said to be effective for some patients, but this does not attend to the underlying personality disorder. Much more research and study are essential. Psychiatry does feel that it can make two well-founded suggestions, however.

First, sexual deviations can be prevented. Children raised by sexually mature parents in reasonably normal homes do not tend to become sexual deviants. This means that we must attempt to structure the lives of today's children so that they become tomorrow's parents in such a manner as to transmit the proper sexual identification to their own offspring. This is easier said then done, and sexual education alone, although it must be the beginning, probably is not the final answer. One of the major problems to the educational approach is that one must first educate the teachers of the children. Sexual education is much more than the transmission of facts about anatomy and physiology.

The hope of total prevention of sexual deviation is utopian and unrealistic. Mankind has not reached the level of maturity necessary to prevent a thing as destructive as war, despite his thousands of years of experience with it. Freud, and others who have studied human behavior, believed that the human has an instinctive drive toward his own destruction. Not all agree with this, but if it should be true, the one effective method of social destruction that probably will remain with us is that of aberrant sexual activity.

The second suggestion, and a more practical one, is that society should drop its punitive attitude toward the sexual deviant. Punitive measures tend to compound and to multiply the already present difficulties of the immature personality. Some deviants who lack control of destructive sexual impulses, such as the rapist and the sadist, do need to be incarcerated for the protection of society, but even this can be done in a humane and constructive manner. Imprisonment or hospitalization without adequate treatment facilities is indefensible in view of our present state of knowledge. It also is detrimental to society in the long run, because it merely makes a hardened and bitter criminal out of an emotionally ill person.

Those deviants who are of no danger to society, such as adult homosexuals, should be no concern of the law. Whatever two adults of consenting age and ability do in private should be legal. This rule allows adequate protection for the underaged and the mentally incompetent. The phrase "in private" protects the public from invasion of its privacy by the exhibitionist, the voyeur, etc. All else should be an individual concern.

Legal and educational alterations will be a good and essential beginning, but a massive social change will be necessary if we are to have a culture that does not wish to exact vengeance. We are a people given to destroying that which does not agree with us or that reminds us too much of our own weaknesses. The witch hunts of Salem are still a very real fact of our heritage, and although we change our witches from time to time, the stern and righteous puritanical streak remains with us.

And yet there are hopeful signs. Repression and suppression of sexuality is steadily becoming less essential, as mentioned in the introduction. Unfortunately this trend has been accompanied by a marked increase in the use of mood changing drugs so that the outcome is obscured. Have we merely substituted a crippling inhibition for an equally crippling freedom? And so the picture becomes confused, and speculation far outweighs good predictive knowledge.

Our judgmental attitude toward the sexual deviant should be framed in the general context of two trite but worthwhile expressions:

"There but for the grace of God go I" and "Let he among you who is without sin. . . ."

Index

Adler, Polly, 159
Adolescent, 9, 10
American Handbook of Psychiatry, 175
Anal Intercourse, 17

Benjamin, Dr. Harry, 86
Berdache, 14, 68
Bisexual, 19
Boston Strangler, 109
Bull Dyke, 18
Butch, 18

Call girl, 167
Child molestation. *See* Pedophilia
Chromosomal gender, 1, 4
  factors in development of, 2
Chromosomes, 2, 86
Coprolalia, 195-96
  case history, 196
  defined, 195
  psychological significance of, 196
Coprophilia, 191-93
  case history, 192-93
  defined, 191
  in prostitution, 121
Cruising, 26
Cunnilingus, 13
  in homosexuality, 17
  in sado-masochism, 115

Daughters of Bilitis, 13
Daughters of Lesbos, 13
De Sade, Marquis, 105-6, 103, 116
Deviation, vii-viii, 10
  behavior patterning in, 11-12
  development of, 1
  as illness, 11-12
  implication of term, 1
  as manifestations of immaturity, 11
  need for social changes toward, 213
  prevention of, 212
  psychopathology of, 210-12
Dildoes. *See* Penis substitutes
Discipline, in group sex, 179

Ellis, Havelock:
  on fetishism, 100
  on group sex, 176
  on sadism, 104
Exhibitionism, 29-40, 41
  case histories, 33-36, 39
  causes, 30-31
  a compulsive condition, 36-37
  defined, 29
  ego-syntonic, 77
  in females, 37-38
  guilt and need for punishment, 36
  homosexual, 32
  legal aspects of, 40
  in polymorphous perversions, 204

psychiatric treatment of, 37
psychodynamics of, 30–32
verbal, 39

Fairy queen, 18
Fellatio, 12, 21, 26
  in rape, 122
Femaleness, 1–2, 4. *See also* Gender
  development of sense of, 6–9
  relationship to core gender, 2
Femininity. *See also* Sexual identification
  concept of, 1–2
  development of attitudes toward, 6–9
  sense of 5, 6
Fetishism, 11, 91–102
  anxiety as factor in, 93
  behavioral therapy in, 102
  case histories, 94–96, 96–99
  defined, 91
  frottage in, 100
  in history, 92–93
  masturbation in, 95
  objects used in, 93–94, 100
  partialism in, 91, 100
  as personality disorder, 101
  personality of fetishist, 93
  sado-masochism in, 97
  without sexual symbolism, 92
  in transvestism, 67, 102
  treatment of, 95–96, 102
Field, Eugene, 7
Freud, Sigmund:
  on human destructive drive, 212
  on incest, 137
  on madonna-prostitute syndrome, 145
  on Oedipal period, 7
  on pedophilia, 56, 62
  on prostitution, 167
  on sado-masochism, 106
  on voyeurism, 44
Frigidity, 10
Frottage, 100

Gender, Core. *See also* Sexual identification
  age of development, 4–5, 7–9
  case history, 2–4
  chromosomal gender, 1–2, 4
  concept defined, 1–2
  external genitalia as sign of, 2
  factors in development of, 2, 6–9
  medical intervention in, 5
  psychological gender, 2
  somatic gender, 2
  transsexualism as disturbance of, 81
Gerontophilia, 203
  defined, 203
  dynamics of, 203
Greek culture, 176
Greek love, 14
Group sex, 175–182
  closed and open swinging, 180
  defined, 175
  factor of madonna-prostitute syndrome in, 158, 185–86
  homosexual elements in, 181, 184–85
  latent homosexuality in, 184
  masturbation in, 182
  methods of heightening pleasure in, 182
  oral-genital activities in, 181
  origins of, 176
  psychodynamics of, 183–84
  publications concerning, 178–79
  sado-masochism in, 179
  as sexual deviation, 186
  social aspects of, 177, 182
  structure in, 180–81
  taboos of, 182–83, 186–87
  voyeurism in, 184

Harlow, Dr. H., 5
  on sexual identification in monkeys, 5
Heterosexuality, 11
Homosexual:
  marriages, 26
  panic, 25
  prostitution, 171–73
  rape, 119–20, 131

Homosexual, continued
  societies, 25
Homosexuality, 4, 6, 8, 11, 13–27
  causes of, 14–15
  defined, 13
  development of tendencies toward, 15–16
  female. *See* Lesbianism
  in group sex, 184
  in history, 13–14
  legal aspects of, 17
  male: case histories, 15–16, 19–22; fear of female in, 26; in group sex, 184; latent, 25; mythology of, 18, 24; overt, 15; sexual practices in, 17
  parental influences on, 15–16
  popular terminology of, 18, 19
  psychiatric treatability of, 25, 27
  psychodynamics of, 25–27
  social aspects of, 17, 27
  in transvestism, 80
House girl, 167

Incest, 133–44
  brother-sister, 134–35
  case histories, 138–41
  defined, 133
  effects on victim, 141
  father-daughter, 134, 136–38
  father's role in, 143
  grandfather-grandchild, 136
  in history, 133–34
  legal aspects of, 133, 144
  madonna-prostitute syndrome in, 145
  mother-son, 135–36
  mother's role in, 141–42
  in Oedipal period, 134, 137
  pedophilia in, 143
  social aspects of, 134
  strength of inclination to, 133
  taboos of, 133
  treatment of, 144
Intercrural intercourse, 57

Jack the Ripper, 109

Jorgensen, Christine, 79

Kama Sutra, 160
Kinsey, Dr., 23, 176
Kipling, Rudyard, 159, 170
Kleptomania, 205–6
  definition of, 205
  sexual components in, 205
  symbolization in, 205

Lady Godiva, 41
Lesbianism, 13. *See also* Homosexuality
  case history, 22–23
  fear of male in, 26
  mythology of, 18
  sexual practices in, 17–18
  social aspects of, 16
  use of penis substitutes in, 17–18
Lesbos, 13
Lolita, 56
Lorenz, Conrad: on sexual identification in animals, 5
Lust murder, 120

Madonna-Prostitute syndrome, 145–58
  case histories, 142–50, 151–53, 155
  child bearing as factor in, 154–55
  defined, 145
  female counterpart, 150–51
  "games" played in, 156–57
  in group sex, 158, 185–86
  in incest, 145
  in mixoscopia, 198
  mother image as factor in, 146–47
  motivations toward, 145–46
  orgasm in, 150
  in Pygmalionism, 197
  treatment of, 158
Maleness, 1–2, 4. *See also* Gender
  development of sense of, 6–9
  relationship to cord gender, 1, 2, 8
Malleus Malfacarum, 104
Masculinity. *See also* Sexual identification
  concept of, 1

development of attitudes toward, 6–9
sense of, 5, 7
Masochism. *See* Sado-Masochism
Masturbation, 21
　in exhibitionism, 32
　in fetishism, 95
　in group sex, 182
　in homosexuality, 12
　in pyromania, 205
　in sado-masochism, 107, 110
　in transvestism, 73, 75, 83–84
　in voyeurism, 42
Mattachine Society, 25
Menarche, 9–10
Mixoscopia, 197–98
　case histories, 197–98
　defined, 197
　in madonna-prostitute syndrome, 198
　voyeurism in, 197–98
Mother, surrogate, 5
Mujerado, 68
Mutual masturbation, 17

Necrophilia, 200–202
　case history, 202
　defined, 200–201
　psychopathology of, 201
　in sado-masochism, 109
　sexual inferiority in, 201
　victims in, 202
Necrophagia, 201
Nymphomania, 11, 198–200
　case history, 199
　defined, 198
　mythology of, 198

One, (organization), 25
Oedipal Period, 7–9
　in gerontophilia, 203
　in incest, 134, 137
　in pedophilia, 56
　in sado-masochism, 111–12, 116
Oral-Genital activities. *See* Cunnilingus; Fellatio
Orgasm, 10
　in fetishism, 101
　in madonna-prostitute syndrome, 150
　in transsexualism, 88

Partialism, 100
Pederasty, 17
Pedophile. *See* Pedophilia
Pedophilia, 11, 53–65, 211
　case histories, 58–61
　defined, 53
　in elderly men, 63–64
　in the female, 53–55
　group therapy as treatment of, 65
　homosexual, 53, 57
　in incest, 143
　legal aspects of, 65
　in polymorphous perversions, 203–4
　psychopathology of, 55
　role of victim in, 63
　victims of, 61–63
Peeping tom. *See* Voyeurism
Penis substitutes:
　in group sex, 118
　in lesbianism, 17–18
Phallic period, 6
Polymorphous perversion, 203–4
　case history, 203–4
　defined, 203
　treatability, 204
Pornography, 193–96
　as aid in masturbation, 193
　case history, 193–94
　defined, 193
　etiology, 195
　psychological significance of, 194
　relationship to sexual crimes, 194–95
Prostitution, 150, 159–93
　aberrant practices in, 171
　case history, 165–66
　defined, 159
　effect of "sexual revolution" on, 170
　factor of drug abuse in, 165
　history of, 160–61
　homosexual prostitution, 171–73
　identity problems in, 170

Index 219

Prostitution, *continued*
  legal aspects of, 173
  in madonna-prostitute syndrome, 150
  motivations of prostitutes, 164–65
  types of prostitutes, 166–69
Puberty, 8, 9
Pygmalionism, 196–97
  defined, 196–97
Pyromania, 204–5
  sexual components in, 204–5

Rape, 119–31
  in association with murder, 120
  case histories, 122–24, 125–26
  defined, 119
  fantasies in, 121
  fellatio in, 122
  gang, 122
  homosexual, 119–20, 131
  motivating factors in, 121–22
  prevention of, 131
  role of alcohol in, 130–31
  role of drugs in, 130–31
  role of female in, 128–29
  as sexual deviation, 120
  statutory, 120
  treatability, 130
Roman culture, 14, 176, 180
Rousseau, Jean Jacques, 29–30, 37

Sacher-Masoch, Leopold, 103, 112–13, 116
Sado-Masochism, 103–118
  behavioral aspects of, 117
  cunnilingus in, 115
  an danger to society, 116
  defined, 103–4
  in fetishism, 97
  in history, 104
  legal aspects of, 117
  masturbation in, 107–10
  necrophilia in, 109
  Oedipal conflict in, 111–16
  in polymorphous perversion, 203
  prevention and treatment of, 117
Sadism: active-passive concepts, 105; case histories, 107–10; developmental factors, 106–7; lust murder in, 109; root in primitive aspect of behavior, 104–5; writings of de Sade, 105–6
Masochism: case histories, 113–16; childhood origins, 111–12; in group sex, 179; as normal female trait, 111; Sacher-Masoch as case history, 1–3, 112–13
Saliromania, 200
  defined, 200
Satyriasis, 11, 198–200
  defined, 199
Sexual activity:
  aim of, 10–11
  drive, 10–11
  need for, 11
  object of, 11, 55
Sexual identification. *See also* Gender, Core
  aspects of, 1, 5–6, 26
  behavior patterning, 11
  development of, 4–6, 7–9
  immature, 11
  maturation of, 10
  in monkeys, 5
  parental role in, 9
Sexual role, 9
Sexual revolution, VII, 170
Sodomy, 17
Stoller, Dr. Robert J.: on transvestism, 69
Street walker, 166
Swinging. *See* Group sex
Switch-hitting, 19

Transsexualism, 4, 79–90
  case histories, 4, 81–85
  conversion surgery, 86, 89, 90
  defined, 79
  as disturbance of core gender, 79, 81
  etiology, 80
  homosexuality in, 80
  hormones in, 88
  legal aspects of, 89

orgasm in, 88
prevention of, 90
treatability, 87
Transvestism, 6, 14, 67-77
 case histories, 72-73, 73-76
 defined, 67
 in females, 68-69, 71
 in history, 67-68
 legal aspects of, 77
 mother's role in, 69-70, 75
 prevention of, 77
 psychoanalytical theory of, 69

Urophilia (urolagnia), 189-91
 case history, 190
 defined, 189

 in polymorphous perversion, 203
 in prostitution, 121
 psychological significance of, 191

Voyeurism, 34, 41-52, 211
 case histories, 44-49, 50-51
 defined, 41
 eyes as aggressive instrument in, 42
 fantasies in, 45-46
 forbidden aspects of, 42-43
 in group sex, 184
 legal aspects of, 52
 in mixoscopia, 197-98
 in polymorphous perversion, 203-4
 psychodynamic concepts of, 44-49
 role of victim, 49